T0233744

Human-Computer Interaction Series

Editors-in-Chief
John Karat

Jean Vanderdonckt
Louvain-la-Neuve, Belgium

HCI is a multidisciplinary field focused on human aspects of the development of computer technology. As computer-based technology becomes increasingly pervasive—not just in developed countries, but worldwide—the need to take a human-centered approach in the design and development of this technology becomes ever more important. For roughly 30 years now, researchers and practitioners in computational and behavioral sciences have worked to identify theory and practice that influences the direction of these technologies, and this diverse work makes up the field of human-computer interaction. Broadly speaking it includes the study of what technology might be able to do for people and how people might interact with the technology. The HCI series publishes books that advance the science and technology of developing systems which are both effective and satisfying for people in a wide variety of contexts. Titles focus on theoretical perspectives (such as formal approaches drawn from a variety of behavioral sciences), practical approaches (such as the techniques for effectively integrating user needs in system development), and social issues (such as the determinants of utility, usability and acceptability).

Titles published within the Human-Computer Interaction Series are included in Thomson Reuters' Book Citation Index, The DBLP Computer Science Bibliography and The HCI Bibliography.

More information about this series at http://www.springer.com/series/6033

Andrea Resmini
Editor

Reframing Information Architecture

 Springer

Editor
Andrea Resmini
Jönköping International Business School
Jönköping
Sweden

ISSN 1571-5035
ISBN 978-3-319-38088-9   ISBN 978-3-319-06492-5 (eBook)
DOI 10.1007/978-3-319-06492-5
Springer Cham Heidelberg New York Dordrecht London

Printed on acid-free paper

Springer is part of Springer Science+Business Media (www.springer.com)

Preface

Information architecture has changed.

When the practice went mainstream in the mid 1990s, library and information science, the core body of knowledge and expertise introduced by pioneers Lou Rosenfeld and Peter Morville, seemed to be all that was necessary. Information architecture was mostly seen as some sort of library science for the Web, largely tackling problems of labeling, categorization, and ordering.

Today, the illusion of the Web as a library and the Internet as a different and separated world have given way to a much more complex scenario. We live in a post-digital world in which digital and physical blend easily, and the Internet is a piece in a larger mechanism where our activities and our use, consumption and production of information happens across multiple contexts through multiple devices and unstable, emergent choreographies.

We moved from the screen to the world, to portable computing, smartphones and ambient devices, and focus has necessarily moved away from the single artifact, the website, to consider the entire product or service ecosystem as a complex, cross-channel information-based beast, some parts of which might not be online or might not even be digital at all.

Information architecture in the mid 2010s is steadily growing into a channel- or medium-aspecific multi-disciplinary framing, with contributions coming in from architecture, urban planning, design and systems thinking, cognitive science, new media, anthropology, that have been heavily reshaping the practice: conversations about labeling, websites, and hierarchies have been replaced by conversations about sense-making, place-making, design, architecture, crossmedia, complexity, embodied cognition, and their application to the architecture of information spaces as places we live in an increasingly larger part of our lives.

The narratives, frameworks, references, approaches and case-studies in the 11 chapters that follow all vastly exceed in scope and complexity whatever was in place in the mid 1990s: all the same, this is still clearly information architecture, concerned with "structuring information spaces", orders, and meaning.

Academia has been struggling to keep up, somewhat failing to offer the closure, reflections and criticisms which are necessary to consolidate operational praxis into a shared and cohesive body of knowledge: this book, presenting contributions from both academics and practitioners as one continuing conversation, is an invitation to acknowledge both the ongoing changes and the mutual dependence between these two camps in the reframing of the field.

Acknowledgments

This book would not be here without the contributions of a rather large group of individuals. Among these, the 42 researchers, educators, and practitioners who attended the 1st Academic-Practitioner Round Table Workshop on "Reframing Information Architecture" that was held as part of the ASIS&T Information Architecture Summit 2013 in Baltimore, Maryland.

Some of the original peer-reviewed contributors declined to participate to the book claiming, I suspect fraudulently, business impediments of all sorts. It seems just fair to list them here anyway, regardless of their succumbing to book stage fright: Jorge Arango, Keith Instone, Matt Nish-Lapidus, Bogdan Stanciu, Simon Norris, thank you for helping kickstart this conversation.

Thanks go out to Richard Hill of ASIS&T for his continuing support to academic involvement within the ASIS&T Information Architecture Summit, and to Kevin Hoffman, co-chair of the ASIS&T Information Architecture Summit 2013. Kevin suggested that a workshop was the best way to engage the community and produce tangible results for further dissemination, and he was right. Vanessa Foss, director of events at ASIS&T, was instrumental in turning that idea into reality. Thanks, Vanessa.

Thanks to all reviewers and referees: Nils Pharo, Stefano Bussolon, Katriina Byström, Stanislaw Skorka, Dorte Madsen, Bertil Carlsson, and the editorial board of the Journal of Information Architecture.

Also thanks to Stacy Surla, whose help in editing parts of this book has been more than precious, and to the Dublin Corps. You guys know how much of what's in here is yours.

Finally thanks to everyone who has been part of the conversation on reframing information architecture so far, and welcome to those who have just joined. We've come a long way, but there's more up ahead: shall we?

Contents

About the Editor

Andrea Resmini is an assistant professor at Jönköping International Business School, in Jönköping, Sweden. Architect, designer, ICT professional since 1989 and information architect since 1999, Andrea holds a MA in Architecture and Industrial Design from the Politecnico di Milano, Italy and a PhD in Legal Informatics from the University of Bologna, Italy.

He is currently the Editor in Chief of the Journal of Information Architecture and a past two-term president of the Information Architecture Institute.

Andrea blogs at andrearesmini.com and tweets at @resmini.

Contributors

Sally Burford University of Canberra, Canberra, Australia

Duane Degler Design for Context, Bethesda, USA

Terence Fenn University of Johannesburg, Johannesburg, South Africa

David Fiorito EPAM, Empathy Lab, Philadelphia, PA, USA

Andrew Hinton The Understanding Group, Ann Arbor, USA

Jason Hobbs University of Johannesburg, Johannesburg, South Africa

Dan Klyn University of Michigan, Ann Arbor, USA

Flávia Lacerda University of Brasilia, Brasilia, Brazil

Mamede Lima-Marques University of Brasilia, Brasilia, Brazil

Roberto Maggi PoiStory, Bologna, Italy

Rita Massacesi Istituto degli Innocenti, Firenze, Italy

David Peter Simon ThoughtWorks, Chicago, USA

Luca Rosati University for Foreigners Perugia, Perugia, Italy

Antonella Schena Istituto degli Innocenti, Firenze, Italy

Thomas Wendt Surrounding Signifiers, New York, USA

Chapter 1
Information Architecture as a Discipline—A Methodological Approach

Flávia Lacerda and Mamede Lima-Marques

Abstract Since the establishment of information architecture (IA) as an area of expertise and research more than a decade ago, its community of scientists and practitioners has been seeking foundations to establish concepts, scope, relations with other disciplines. Some are motivated by the conceptual gap; others are also concerned about the lack of communication between theory and practice in the field. Attempting to find a scientific method to investigate questions arisen from information architecture, we suggest in this article the adoption of the Meta-Modeling Methodology (M^3) by Van Gigch and Pipino (Future Comput Syst 1:71–97, 1986). We believe it can provide a comprehensive way to understand information architecture as a discipline, promote critical thinking and improve grounded discussions in the community.

1.1 The Meta-Modeling Methodology (M^3)

Van Gigch and Pipino (1986) conceived M^3 as a systemic framework to understand scientific objects and innovation processes. They originally proposed it in the context of information systems, but it has since been applied to other disciplines—see for example Van Gigch (1997), Eriksson (1998), Van Gigch (2003), and Olsson and Sjöstedt (2006).

M^3 comprises three hierarchical levels of inquiry (Van Gigch and Pipino 1986):

- **Meta level (epistemology)**: it represents the conceptual framework of a scientific community. Seeks to investigate the source of the knowledge of the discipline, justify their methods of reasoning and articulate its methodology. It is where innovation, creativity and paradigm shifts occur.
- **Object level (science)**: it presents theories and models to describe, explain and predict problems and their solutions.
- **Application level (practice)**: where practitioners apply the tools (theories, models, techniques and technologies) to solve everyday problems.

F. Lacerda (✉) · M. Lima-Marques
University of Brasilia, Brasilia, Brazil
e-mail: flavialacerdaoliveira@gmail.com

A. Resmini (ed.), *Reframing Information Architecture,* Human-Computer Interaction Series, 1
DOI 10.1007/978-3-319-06492-5_1, © Springer International Publishing Switzerland 2014

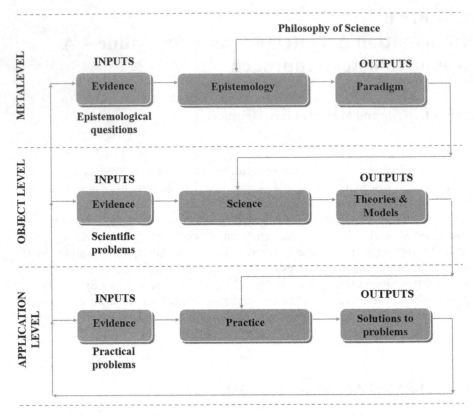

Fig. 1.1 M³ Hierarchy of inquiring systems. (Adapted from Van Gigch and Pipino 1986)

Figure. 1.1 illustrates the hierarchy of scientific systems within M³ and their inter-relationships. According to the schema, epistemological questions are formulated based on input coming from philosophy of science framings, and on evidence from the scientific and practical levels. Similarly, the scientific level receives input from paradigms identified in the upper meta-level, and from evidences emerging in the practical level. Real-life problems, in turn, are addressed by theories and models in the scientific level and are also a source of evidence to be investigated in the other levels.

Epistemology establishes requirements to consider disciplines as scientific. Despite the lack of consensus on any demarcation criteria, it is possible to identify general characteristics. First, "a field requires a paradigm which provides direction to its inquiry." Paradigms, according to Kuhn (1970), are "universally recognized scientific achievements that, for a time, provide model problems and solutions for a community of researchers." They guide and orient the fundamental definitions of a discipline, such as the object of study and body of knowledge; the disciplinary boundaries and applications; the scientific community and main schools of thought; the purposes, and methodologies to achieve them; and what anomalies and unsolved problems remain. The M^3 method intends to clarify a field's paradigm in order to: (1) integrate the many different perspectives associated with it; (2) generate viable research directions; (3) provide a basis for the comparative analysis of its objects of study; and (4) formulate firm foundations for the discipline to support its practice (Van Gigch and Pipino 1986).

1.2 Information Architecture as a Scientific Discipline

A bibliographical review on information architecture's literature shows a large number of practical or applicative approaches. Publications focused on fundamentals are less common. However, a certain number of works concerned with how information architecture fulfills the scientific requirements presented can be found. Siqueira (2012), for example, aimed to define the discipline of "architecture of information" based on M^3 and criteria settled mainly by Kuhn (1970), Lakatos (1970), Hübner (1986), Popper (1993) and Hempel (2001).

Without the pretension to be comprehensive or exhaustive, we provide here an outline of the relevant elements that can be used to describe information architecture as a discipline.

1.3 Information Architecture has a Specific and Relevant Object of Study

In a wider approach, we could consider the design of information spaces and its social, cultural and technological aspects as information architecture's main object of interest. We agree with those within the community who assert that the information architecture community itself should focus on the essence of its object, to maintain its relevance independently of any context or technological changes. It is critical to avoid technical determinism and avoid framings that would limit information architecture to specific, technology bounded, information spaces, such as the Web as it is currently.

In his World IA Day 2012 presentation, thematic chair Jorge Arango (2012) compared information architecture's essence to the I Ching hexagram "The Well," stating: "Information Architecture is not tied to a particular technology. While it is true that this is a field born from the Internet, information is all around us (...) Information Architecture has always been about help people find and understand things—that is where [information architecture] adds value to the world."

This take goes all the way back to Dillon original distinction between "Big IA" and "Little IA" (2002), with the former pushing "a much more ambitious agenda. It assumes that information spaces need designing on multiple levels and that the user experience of life in that space is a direct concern of the information architect." In that same year, also offering a broad stance, Dale declared "as a discipline, information architecture clearly displays the emergent properties of a complex system. Whilst many of the components that contribute to the field are well understood in isolation, their combination gives rise to new patterns and principles" (Dale 2002). Haverty suggested a concurrent scenario when she wrote that "maybe the body of knowledge that makes information architecture a discipline would be a collection of design patterns that could be reused, depending on the situation" (2002).

Creating a common vocabulary and keeping core concepts consistent and coherent is a significant challenge to the field. Hinton (2013) believes that the lack of consensually well-defined concepts "has contributed in many ways to a years-long circular discourse about what information architecture is and does, preventing (the area) for having a central shared domain as a community of practice that can properly evolve into a full-fledged discipline".

> The search for adequate epistemological elements for engineering a solid foundation for the scientific explanations within (…) AI [Architecture of Information] is crucial. Positioning oneself as regards matters of the core elements (data, information and knowledge) is very complex not only due to the high level of polysemy their usage comprises but also due to what is described by Floridi (2004) and revised by Crnkovic and Hofkirchner (2011) as unsolved problems. Such positioning is, however, fundamental for building coherent scientific theories and developing advanced (Lima-Marques 2011).

Van Gigch (1990) maintains that "a discipline can survive only when (its) respective contributions are integrated into a larger whole where the parts feed into each other. To remove fallacies and avoid paradoxes, it is imperative to use not only the appropriate logic but also the appropriate language."

1.4 Information Architecture is Inherently Transdisciplinary

Information architecture is established in a context where the values of universality and certainty have given place to plurality and complexity. Thus, its nature is inherently transdisciplinary, and its methods, models and theories are strongly influenced by or even derived from a number of external sources and disciplines, including information science, architecture, design, ergonomics, usability, computer science, business administration, philosophy, cognitive science, and linguistics, to cite a few.

This dialogue between disciplines is extremely positive and enriching, since it is based on reciprocity and an alignment of foundations. As defined by Jean Piaget at an OECD workshop (1970), "transdisciplinarity" is an subsequent stage that evolves from interdisciplinarity, "not (…) limited to recognize the interactions and/or reciprocities between the specialized researches, but which will locate these links inside a total system without stable boundaries between the disciplines" (Nicolescu 2010). For Gibbons et al. (1994), "transdisciplinarity arises only if research is based upon a common theoretical understanding and must be accompanied by a mutual interpenetration of disciplinary epistemologies".

Due to these complex dynamics, we can perceive the rise of conflicts among information architecture academics and practitioners, and between representatives of the multiple disciplines involved with its object of study, all bringing their own different relevance and expertise.

In the case of information architecture, we could say that while we have *information* as the raw material, embedded in *objects* delimited by *spaces* intentionally *designed* in order to promote *user experiences* as the core expertise practiced and researched within the field, the multiple disciplines that coalesce around information architecture are certainly all contributing to this artifact, but they highlight different aspects of it: information itself, the objects, the spaces, the design, or the user experience. The multiple points of view should complement each other and provide a richer final artifact. Van Gigch (1993) writes:

> it is difficult to anticipate clearly today which disciplines will be at the forefront of world thinking tomorrow. It is a fact that scientific disciplines also change their names and continue their existence in the context of another newer metadiscipline. The point that needs to be remembered is that a scientific discipline must always refer to its metalevel inquiring system, where the struggle among competing disciplines and paradigms takes place.

1.5   Information Architecture has a Community of Researchers and Practitioners

The establishment of a scientific community is one of the criteria stated by Kuhn (1970) as necessary to characterize a discipline. In the case of information architecture, it is possible to identify a group of people with common interests, focused on teaching and researching questions of a similar nature, meeting regularly at events dedicated to the subject, who recognize the existence of something called "information architecture", and that often call themselves "information architects" or that have that as a job title.

Academic and professional training also takes place around the world. However, there is clearly a need to strengthen the information architecture community to better structure and formalize the area: as many other fields related to technological innovation, information architecture faces an obstacle in the different timing that practice and academia follow, in how they perceive context changes and react to them.

In her still relevant article, Haverty (2002) notes "when we think about how fast information architecture is changing right now (especially considering developments in new technologies (…)), change may be so rapid that the mode of agreement about which solutions work may need to be a consensus within the community rather than the establishment of a theory."

Hobbs et al. (2010) acknowledge the importance for practice to be guided by a stronger and better rounded discipline, pointing out the main problems caused by the shortcoming of consistency in the field:

> (t)he informal structures of a community of practice are limited in their ability to store and
> disseminate knowledge; the validation of knowledge is not rigorous; opinion and knowl-
> edge are often confused; communities of practice tend to be impermanent; there is a lack of
> real progress made in ongoing discourses (discussions are circular); and for the practitioner
> there is no larger coherent body of validated, scientific knowledge to appeal to or apply
> when designing in commercial or other contexts where the designer is accountable.

Resmini and Instone (2010) emphasize how this process requires better bridges
between practitioners and academics, with one party aggregating systematic tests
on the applicability of research and, in turn, with the other developing a more critical analysis of the artifacts produced by the community, "in a way that benefits the
field at large and that produces factual and theoretical knowledge to be reused."
This is precisely the type of interactions between levels within the M^3 cycle that Van
Gigch and Pipino (1986) consider absolutely necessary, a conversation across the
three layers of inquiry—epistemological, scientific and practical—which should be
promoted in order to maintain relevance and innovation in a given area.

To be purposeful, a discipline "may dissolve the polarities of theory and practice, embraced, and comprehended by finding the essence of their commonalities,
instead of emphasizing their differences, which prevents us from capturing the essence of what we are attempting to learn" (Van Gigch and Pipino 1986). This seems
to be echoed by Resmini et al. (2009) who conclude that "an analytical approach
must be taken on the way the community sees itself, with some critical thinking and
some historical perspective. The community needs to grow roots."

1.6 Information Architecture Plays a Significant and Necessary Role in Society

Our society is increasingly an information society. Dillon (2002) wrote that "regardless of how the field eventually becomes labeled (…) the information domain will
be as much the province of architecture as the physical world, and those that will
shape the new spaces will impact humankind on a level that will prove beyond the
reach of physical architecture".

Concerns about any future effects of designing information spaces and the role
of information architecture in this context are hence extremely relevant. Information architecture should be seen as a creative process of transformation, and information architects should be conscious of the social impact of their interventions. As
Salvo (2004) eloquently writes,

> (a)rchitectural design shapes cities and communities and thereby shapes the institutions they
> house and the people that inhabit designed structures. The design of digital environments,
> asserted Wurman (1997), is no less influential on the actions supported and suppressed
> in those virtual spaces. Articulating relationships between different units of information,
> creating paths through oceans of data, and retrieval of hard-won knowledge characterize
> the constructive and powerful influence design has on virtual spaces. The design of these
> virtual spaces is no less influential in constructing relationships than is architecture in con-
> structing physical space.

1.7 Information Architecture is Experiencing a New Context and is Being Reframed

We are witnessing a growing convergence between physical and digital spaces. The most concrete manifestation of this phenomenon is the so-called "Internet of Things." Information is being embedded in commonly used objects everywhere, and their networked existence creates ubiquitous information spaces. We believe that this is fundamentally changing the way we understand information architecture: the way we deal with its challenges in scientific terms and, definitely, the way we practice it. As Morville wrote in the foreword for Resmini and Rosati "Pervasive Information Architecture" (2011), "How do we rise to the new challenges of creating paths and places that bridge physical, digital and cognitive spaces?"

More fundamental questions arise from this context: Are we facing a paradigm shift? Does information architecture has theories and models to explain and address emerging issues? Which disciplinary fields could be influential and what can we learn from them—Design, Architecture, Cognitive Sciences?

The information architecture community is expanding its worldviews, its scope of action, and its motivations, as a string of public talks by Morville (2012), Arango (2012), Resmini (2013), Hinton (2013), and Klyn (2013), among others, clearly show. These urgency to redefine the boundaries invests publications, social networks, and events worldwide—the round table workshop on "Reframing Information Architecture" at the ASIS &T IA Summit 2013 in Baltimore, USA, whose intended goal was to "move the conversation forward, consolidate intuitions into discipline, and help establish a common language and grammar for both practice and research in the field" and which led to this book; or the 4th Colloquium on the Architecture of Information promoted by the Centre for Research on Architecture of Information at the University of Brasília, Brazil, in 2012.

> Calling for an epistemological renewal means asking the scholars of the discipline to elevate themselves to the metalevel inquiring system, in order to question some of the presently held approaches. The production of lasting innovative work will signal the advent of a new paradigm or, at least, the modification of the existing one (Van Gigch 1990).

1.8 Conclusions

We introduced the Meta-Modeling Methodology (M^3) as a systemic framework to better approach information architecture as a discipline. The methodology allows to analyze and structure knowledge in the field and about the field around three consecutive levels of inquiry—epistemology, science, and practice—whose interactions promote advancement and critical reflections on theories, methods and applications.

Maintaining a balanced system that harmonically furthers all planes and the interrelations between them is essential to foster a consistent development in the field. We also addressed the disciplinary nature of information architecture in respect to Kuhn's (1970) notions of what constitutes a scientific discipline, and argued that:

- **Information architecture has a specific and relevant object of study**: the design of information spaces and its social, cultural and technological aspects. However, the area should consolidate a body of knowledge and address epistemological and scientific issues, in order to establish foundations, align concepts, and develop clearer purposes together with efficient methods to achieve them. Technical determinism and limitation of scope are unwarranted.
- **Information architecture is inherently transdisciplinary**, and its dialogue with related disciplines is a healthy and enriching conversation, provided that reciprocity and foundational alignments, both in language and scope, are in place, so that circular reasoning and opinion-as-fact controversies can be avoided.
- **Information architecture has a growing and prolific group of scholars and practitioners** often acknowledged as "information architects", who are keeping the dialogue alive in events and publications, and are assuming or have assumed leading positions in both academia and the practice. However, academia and the practice still conduct a fragmented and sometimes difficult, misaligned conversation.
- **Information architecture plays a significant and necessary role in society**, and information architects must be conscious about the social impact of their interventions—how they influence people's lives through the unveiling of patterns, the anticipation of behaviors, and the careful design of structures of content that promote experiences.
- **Information architecture is experiencing a new context of framing with the rise of ubiquitous information spaces** that connect people, objects and information everywhere they are. These are potentially transformative spaces to act in, but, as well as physical spaces, they must be architected to meet human needs.

In this quest for the scientific foundations of information architecture, we should keep in mind Lévi-Strauss insight (1969) on the challenge that all scientists face, that of asking the "right questions, rather than the right answers". The rethinking of information architecture is timely and necessary. While reflecting on the sociocultural and technological implications that affect all dimensions of this new blended reality that remixes physical and digital seamlessly is not only information architecture's duty, some questions would go unanswered without its contribution.

References

Arango, J. (2012). World Information Architecture Day 2012 Keynote. http://www.youtube.com/watch?v=kY5CC2QfevE. Accessed Dec 2013.

Crnkovic, G. D.; Hofkirchner, W. (2011). Floridi's "open problems in philosophy of information", ten years later. Information, 2(2), 327–359.

Dale, A. (2002). Letter 12: Information architecture: The next professional battleground? Journal of Information Science, 28(6), 523–525. (http://cat.inist.fr/?aModele=afficheN&cpsidt=14402115).

Dillon, A. (2002). Information architecture in JASIST: Just where did we come from? Journal of the American Society for Information Science and Technology, 10(53), 821–823.

Eriksson, D. M. (1998). *Managing problems of postmodernity: Some heuristics for evaluation of systems approaches (Working Paper)*. International Institute for Applied Systems Analysis. http://ideas.repec.org/p/wop/iasawp/ir98060.html.

Floridi, L. (2004). Open problems in the philosophy of information. Metaphilosophy, Blackwell Publishing, *35*(4), 554–582. Accessed July 2004.

Gibbons, M., Limoges, C., Nowotny, H., Schwartzman, S., Scott, P., & Trow, M. (1994). *The new production of knowledge: The dynamics of science and research in contemporary societies*. London: Sage.

Haverty, M. (2002). Information architecture without internal theory: An inductive design process. *Journal of the American Society for Information Science and Technology, 10*(53), 839–845.

Hinton, A. (2013). *A model for information environments*. Reframing information architecture. Workshop at the ASIS & T IA Summit 2013. http://www.slideshare.net/andrewhinton/a-model-for-information-environments-reframe-ia-workshop-2013.

Hempel, C. G. (2001). The Philosophy of Carl G. Hempel: studies in Science, Explanation and Rationality. New York: Oxford University Press.

Hobbs, J., Fenn, T., & Resmini, A. (2010). Maturing a practice. *Journal of Information Architecture, 2*(1), 37–54. (http://journalofia.org/volume2/issue1/04-hobbs/).

Hübner, K. (1986). Crítica da Razão Científica. 3. ed. Lisboa: Edições 70, 1986. (O Saber da Filosofia).

Klyn, D. (2013). *Dutch uncles, ducks and decorated sheds*. Reframing Information Architecture. ASIS & T IA Summit 2013. http://www.slideshare.net/danfnord/dutch-uncles-ducks-and-decorated-sheds-reframing-ia.

Kuhn, T. S. (1970). *The structure of scientific revolutions*. Chicago: University of Chicago Press.

Lakatos, I. (1970). Falsification and the methodology of scientific research programs. Cambridge: Cambridge University Press, 1970. cap. 6.

Lévi-Strauss, C. (1969). *Mythologiques*. Chicago: University of Chicago Press.

Lima-Marques, M. (2011). Outline of a theoretical framework of architecture of information: A school of Brasilia proposal. In Beziau, J.-Y. & Coniglio, M. E. (Eds.), *Logic without frontiers. Festschrift for Walter Alexandre Carnielli on the occasion of his 60th birthday*. London: College Publications.

Morville, P. (2012). World Information Architecture Day 2012. http://www.youtube.com/watch?v=C8o-IPBvS2k.

Nicolescu, B. (2010). Methodology of transdisciplinarity–levels of reality, logic of the included middle and complexity. *Transdisciplinary Journal of Engineering & Science, 1*(1), 18–37.

Olsson, M.-O., & Sjöstedt, G. (2006). *Systems approaches and their application: Examples from Sweden*. Berlin: Springer.

Popper, K. R. (1993). A Lógica da Pesquisa Científica. 4. ed. São Paulo: Editora Cultrix, 1993.

Resmini, A. (2013). *Ghosts in the machine*. Opening keynote. WIAD 2013 Bristol. http://www.slideshare.net/resmini/ghosts-in-the-machine-16512059.

Resmini, A., Byström, K., & Madsen, D. (2009). IA Growing Roots: Concerning the Journal of IA. Bulletin of the American Society for Information Science and Technology, *35*(3). Retrieved from http://www.asis.org/Bulletin/Feb-09/FebMar09_Resmini_Bystrom_Madsen.html.

Resmini, A., & Instone, K. (2010). Research and practice in IA. *Bulletin of the Association for Information Science and Technology*. http://www.asis.org/Bulletin/Aug-10/AugSep10_Resmini_Instone.html

Resmini, A., & Rosati, L. (2011). *Pervasive information architecture: Designing cross-channel user experiences*. Massachusetts: Morgan Kaufmann.

Salvo, M. J. (2004). Rhetorical action in professional space information architecture as critical practice. *Journal of Business and Technical Communication, 18*(1), 39–66. (http://jbt.sagepub.com/content/18/1/39).

Siqueira, A. H. de. (2012). *Arquitetura da informação: uma proposta para a fundamentação e caracterização de uma disciplina científica*. Faculdade de Ciência da Informação. Universidade de Brasília, Brasília.

Van Gigch, J. P. (1990). Systems science, the discipline of epistemological domains, contributes to the design of the intelligent global web. *Behavioral Science,* 35(2), 122. (http://onlinelibrary. wiley.com/doi/10.1002/bs.3830350205/abstract).

Van Gigch, J. P. (1993). Metamodeling: The epistemology of system science. *System Practice and Action Research,* 6(3), 8.

Van Gigch, J. P. (1997). The design of an epistemology for the management discipline which resolves dilemmas among ethical and other imperatives. *System Practice,* 10(4), 14.

Van Gigch, J. P. (2003). The paradigm of the science of management and of the management science disciplines. *Systems Research and Behavioral Science,* 20, 449–506.

Van Gigch, J. P., & Pipino, L. L. (1986). In search of a paradigm for the discipline of information systems. *Future Computer System,* 1(1), 71–97.

Wurman, R. S. (1997). Information Architects. 2. ed. Lakewood: Watson-Guptill Pubns, 1997. 240 p.

Chapter 2
The Information Architecture of Meaning Making

Terence Fenn and Jason Hobbs

Abstract We live in a world of increasingly complex, interconnected, societal problems. Design Thinking (DT), as an academic concern, and amongst other disciplines, has been grappling with such problems since the 1970s in order to solve the problems facing humanity and the environment. Initially, this paper briefly introduces the discourse of design thinking before describing in reference to selected theory from the field of design thinking a brief account of the characteristics of complexity and indeterminacy within the design phases of *researching*, *ideation* and *prototyping*. This paper then examines the ways in which the practice of information architecture (information architecture, IA) operates in some very similar ways and how this view reframes an understanding of the practice of IA. The paper will then present three 'illusions' embedded in the current view of information architecture that we believe account for its misconception. The reframing of IA presented here has implications for the field of information architecture, its theory, its practice and the teaching thereof, but perhaps more importantly also for other fields of design that stand to gain enormous value from the application of the thinking, tools and techniques of IA to grapple with the complex problems of our time.

2.1 Introduction

In the past decade many of the disciplines traditionally described as design, including graphic design, industrial design, and information design, have undergone a conceptual shift that has seen them transformed from practices primarily focused with surface, form and product to become fundamentally concerned with solving problems facing humanity and the environment. This reframing of design has led to a number of significant changes that have and continue to impact design practice and design education.

This reconsideration of design has been highly influenced by the discourse of and about design thinking. While design thinking (DT) has in recent times been ad-

T. Fenn (✉) · J. Hobbs
University of Johannesburg, Johannesburg, South Africa
e-mail: tfenn@uj.ac.za

A. Resmini (ed.), *Reframing Information Architecture*, Human-Computer Interaction Series, 11
DOI 10.1007/978-3-319-06492-5_2, © Springer International Publishing Switzerland 2014

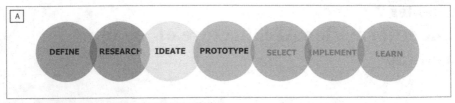

Paul Harris & Gavin Ambrose. 2009. Basic Design: Design Thinking

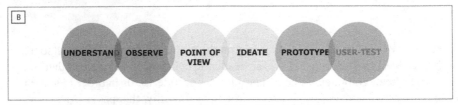

Uli Weinwer. 2009. Design Thinking process. HPI School of Design Thinking, Universitat Potsdam

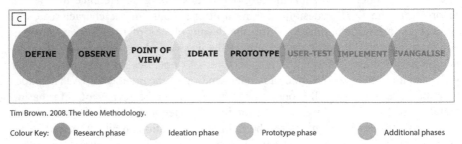

Tim Brown. 2008. The Ideo Methodology.

Colour Key:　●　Research phase　　　○　Ideation phase　　　●　Prototype phase　　　●　Additional phases

Fig. 2.1 An illustration of 3 design thinking models from Harris and Ambrose, Weiner and Brown respectively

vocated as an approach to generating innovative business practice[1], DT has a legacy in design theory that can be traced back at least as far as the early 1970s. There is a however strong cross-pollination between the business process driven approach and the more theoretical discursive approach. Between these two polarities, DT as the applied practice of design that seeks to solve the problems facing humanity and the environment is enacted.

As reflected in Fig. 2.1, DT is often represented diagrammatically as a model detailing a continuum of phases representing the design process. Each phase reflects a particular mode of conceptual activity and the continuum is understood as iteratively self-regulating. In Fig. 2.1, model A originates from Paul Harris and Gavin Ambrose's *Basic Design: Design Thinking* (2009) model B is adapted from Potsdam D-school's model (Weiner 2009), and model C is an adaption of the IDEO model (Brown 2008). Although all the models have at times differently named stages, they are at an overall level conceptually similar in that the *Prototype* phase can be considered to be preceded by *Ideation* and *Research* phases.

The concern of this paper is not to exhaustively define a model for DT but rather to use the various DT models to present the sequence of conceptual thinking in a

---

[1] See Thomas Lockwood's Design Thinking: Integrating Innovation, Customer Experience, and Brand Value (2010) for a business orientated description of design thinking.

generic DT design process so that the acts of synthetic conceptualisation that occur within the *Ideation* phase and are required for the transformation of *Research* into *Prototype* may be contextualised. For it is within the *Ideation* phase that the designer grapples with complexity in an attempt to resolve, through the artificial, a solution to the problem and it is here, we feel, that information architecture may be able to assist the designer to cognitively construct resolution.

2.2 Research in Design Thinking

The *Research* phase of DT is concerned with understanding the societal world within which the final design solution will exist and operate. For as Klaus Krippendorff suggests in *Design Research: an Oxymoron* (2007), design is inherently a social activity and thus in order to produce meaningful solutions, a designer must acknowledge and support peoples conceptions and desires and this requires listening, observing and collaborating with people so as to understand how they "think and justify their actions in worlds they always are in the process of constructing".

Design research[2] is at the most fundamental level, the practice of collecting information about users and their physical and conceptual environments so as to gain a holistic understanding of the design problem and the social circumstance from which the problem arose. Research methods that are used to extract this information vary in range but include examples such as user and group interviews, observation; user probes diaries and contextual mapping. Conducting design research can be in itself multifaceted. As far back as the early 1970s, Horst Rittel and Melvin Webber, in *Dilemmas in a General Theory of Planning (1973)*, describe the difficulties of identifying societal problems:

> We have been learning to see social processes as the links tying up open systems into large and interconnected network of systems, such that outputs of one become inputs of another. In that structural framework it has become less apparent where problem centers lie, and less apparent where and how we should intervene even if we know what aims we seek.

Richard Buchannan in *Wicked Problems* (1992) further propagates the value of research as he believes the act of designing should be orientated around attempting to understand the societal problem as he considers the fundamental activity of design as the conceptualization and development of solutions purely in response to the contexts of the particular problem at hand.

The outcome of a rigorous and rich research exploration into social reality results in complexity, as social reality is inexhaustibly intricate. At its most tangible, the complexity takes the form of data generated by the research activities. It is worth noting that the research data can only ever be interpretive as according to Bourdieu (Highmore 2008), social reality is itself regulated by the 'proclivities and dispositions, the abilities, practices and understandings that are often only tacitly understood' and the selection of what is valued is based on the decision making of

---

[2] The term 'design research' is used inclusively to describe any human-centered design research practice that informs the design processes and is not meant to represent either Plomp and Nieveen's '*Educational Design Research*' (2009) or Koskinen et al.'s (2011) '*Design Research*' methodology.

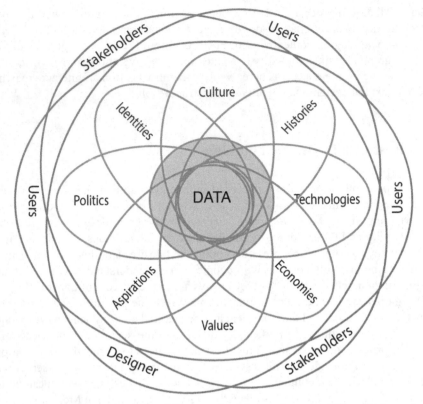

Fig. 2.2 Illustrates examples of the different societal factors that potentially could be explored, across the numerous stakeholders, in order to begin to address societal problems

the researcher and what is divulged by members of the society. Research data that reflects the complexities of people's lives can be understood to impact on the design process in two distinct but entwined ways. Firstly, the data originating from the research process can be understood as the context from which the problem emerges and secondly, also as the context that provides the relational social logic that the solution must acknowledge in order to seem 'spontaneous' (Highmore 2008) to the end user community. In this essay, we refer to the rich complexity that is reflected by research data as a *problem ecology* (Fig. 2.2).

2.3 Ideation in Design Thinking

Rittel and Webber (1973) connect the act of understanding and the act of forming design in a mutual relationship. They describe the requirements of design problem solving as follows:

> One cannot understand the problem without knowing about its context; one cannot meaningfully search for information without the orientation of a solution concept; one cannot first understand, then solve.

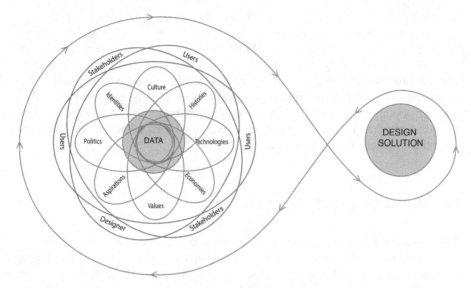

Fig. 2.3 A representation of a problem and solution conjecture

Rittel and Webber place both the context of the problem and any potential solution within an iterative loop that cyclically and reciprocally edits the understanding of both as illustrated in Fig. 2.3. This iterative loop is in essence the *Ideation* phase of the design process and attempts to reconcile the research findings with the artificial solution in a problem/solution conjecture. Therefore, if the resulting complexity from the research is manifested as data, then the process of 'understanding' the data through synthesis can be considered essential in the act of problem resolution.

Nigel Cross (2006) observes that this type of problem/solution conjecture as typical of the thinking employed by designers, as designers are 'solution-focused'. Cross and Dorst (in Cross 2006) describe the stages of defining mutual problems and solutions as follows:

> The designer starts by exploring the [problem space], and find, discover, or recognize a partial structure. That partial structure is then used to provide them also with a partial structuring of the [solution space]. They consider the implication of the partial structure within the solution space, use it to generate some initial ideas for the form of a design concept, and so extend the partial structuring... They transfer the developed partial structure back into the [problem space] and again consider implications and extending the structuring of the [problem space]. Their goal.... Is to create a matching problem-solution pair

Thus the formulation of matching problem-solutions is a conceptual process during which design solutions emerge from the designer's analysis, categorization, structuring, organization prioritization and consideration of the rich data. The emergent solution, selected by the designer, then reciprocally further reduces the range of relevant data, focusing on the data that will impact further thinking around the solution. For example, if a problem ecology was constructed around 'city transport' data describing perceptions of automobile wear and tear could be discarded once the strategic decision to build cheap bicycles and develop safer cycle routes has taken place. This iterative, conceptual repositioning of problem and solutions can be described as the generation of design solutions by reducing the complexity though analysis while simultaneously forming meaning (the solution) through synthetic construction[3]. Additionally, we contend that the problem/solutions conjectures can be viewed in a less binary structure then Cross's 'pairs' as a problem could, after consideration, be better understood to have a number of equally acceptable solutions depending on specific contexts and users. Alternatively, problems may also require a system of solutions. For example the problem of 'crime' could be solved by finding solutions for problems as diverse as poor education, lack of employment, cultural entitlement and police corruption.

2.4   Prototyping in Design Thinking

How Cross and Dorst's (in Cross 2006) *'partial structure'* in the problem/solution conjuncture is manifested is crucial in understanding one of the primary distinguishing features of the DT approach to problem solving. In DT the design solution evolves from the partial structure, which in turn evolves from data collected in the human-centered research exploration. The design solution can thus be considered to have emerged from a 'bottom up' or generative approach within which there is a clear conceptual link between research insights gained from people, and the final solution.

This framing of design contrasts with a product-led, more traditionally view of design within which the various disciplines of design each have their own product types. These product types can be regarded as generic solutions that have been developed over time and have been successfully proven to be adept at solving particular determinate problems. For example the design product 'chair' is a proven solution for the problem 'what do I put in the living room to facilitate rest?' Subsequently, in most Industrial Design departments, at one stage or another, students are briefed to design a chair.

The power of the design product is that their value has been established and proven through their usefulness. This power is also the design products weakness as meaning is often 'hidden' in the product itself, contextual rather than universal and often tied into socio-political systems that may be culturally, economically and ecologically unsustainable. For example, in traditional African cultures where mats are used to sit on, is the answer to 'what do I put in the living room to facilitate rest?' still a chair? In reality the concept of 'chair' fits into a larger perhaps Western concept of 'sitting room', which fits into an idea of a space for rest, and everything seems to make sense. But in a village without lounges, that have different understandings of resting and different practices, spaces and rituals for rest, the concept of 'chair' may appear bizarre.

---

[3] See Dindler (2010) for a discussion of the historical emergence in design theory of problem setting and problem solutioning.

Buchanan (1992) counsels against the temptation of applying premeditated and assumptive[4] design solutions to complex problems. Buchannan describes the results of this dependence as "mannered imitations of an earlier invention" that may no longer be relevant to the specific possibilities of a new situation. Applying design products automatically in response to design problems, without a rigorous investigation into the nature of the problem, implies that design problems all share the same problem data set and are consistently alike. Nigel Cross (2006) similarly describes product-led approaches, which he terms 'fixation', as a phenomenon that limits particularly inexperienced designers to "reuse features of existing designs rather than explore the problem and generate new features" as problematic.

Johann van der Merwe (2010) in a *Natural Death is Announced* describes design as a discipline-neutral groundless field of knowledge that constantly sources knowledge, skills, practices and contexts from other fields of knowledge as dictated by the location of the 'specific design problem' Van der Merwe's observation implies that design solutions are in their own manner as indeterminate as design problems and contain no natural form or structure and are always acts of synthetic construction.

The framing of the design process to include complexity and indeterminacy during problem formation (*Research* phase) and during solution formation (*Prototype* phase), while acknowledging the interrelated systemic nature of design problems and design solutions, has lead us to use, in this essay, the phrase 'the problem/solution ecology' to describe the *Ideation* phase. Key characteristics of problem/solution ecologies include, amongst other things, paradox, conflict and contradiction and this is where a traditionally analytic approach to solutioning falls short as do often purely discipline-led approaches as they fail to grasp the larger complexities of the problem wherein paradox, conflict and contradiction often reside. Attempting to better understand the problem ecology through analysis, categorization, structuring, organization prioritization and reflection often provides clarity, new perspectives and creates opportunities to reconfigure solutions by restructuring the problem.

2.5   The Practice of Information Architecture

Although the term "information architecture" was first applied by Richard Saul Wurman, an architect, in his book *Information Architects* (1997) the practice of information architecture tends not to be associated with "design" but rather an adaptation and evolution of thinking, tools and techniques (for example taxonomies, common in the field) derived from fields such as Information and Library Science. This is in no small part due to the usefulness of the thinking in these fields in dealing with data storage and retrieval challenges so relevant to information rich environments such as the World Wide Web.

Remaining true to Wurman's thinking on information architecture the term remains applied in graphic design and information design practices where its applica-

---

[4] Buchanan terms these types of solutions as 'categorical'.

tion refers to the structuring of the visual representation of information, predominantly in print media. The term can also be found applied in the field of information technology (IT) where it refers to the flow, storage, rules and relationships of data in IT architecture.

Our interest in this paper however is oriented to the practice of information architecture as applied primarily in media spaces rather than IT and in particular the way that the practice has come to be understood as falling within the field of user experience design (UXD) (Hobbs et al. 2010). In this reading UXD has a primary focus on digital environments (like the World Wide Web) where the practice of information architecture design is one of several practices that contribute to the design and production of interactive experiences like websites. These practices include but are not limited to interaction design, usability, copywriting, art direction, coding and programming, etc.

Earlier in this paper we described the manner in which DT operates to solve complex, indeterminate problems situated in social reality. Similarly to DT, information architects either research to discover or are provided with large amounts of research data, which they organize such that it can be understood, and in so doing present a solution. This maps to the first two stages in DT (Research and Ideation) and again, like DT, information architects produce prototypes that can be tested and iterated upon by reference back to research and users.

Information architecture also shares with DT a view of problems as systemic. Information architecture, when practiced, is most often solution focused and applies models of research, organization and feedback to understand and explore the system or systems in which the problem exists. Information architecture methodologies and solutions are understood to be transient, iterative and evolving, as users and context are better understood and change over time.

2.6   Research in Information Architecture

The practice of information architecture today is predominantly product-led where solutions are required for specific channel bound problems. For example, companies often find that users cannot find the information they require promptly or effectively on websites and will turn to information architects to re-organise and/or re-label content and sections to improve the findability of content. The reasons why users struggle to find specific items of content or functionality can vary broadly however: websites, for example, exist in the context of the broader media mix and channel make up of companies where differing organizational logics may apply in different channels or contexts. This can create an expectation by a user that a consistent logic will be applied and when it does not, results in findability problems. Equally, a user's mental model may not map to a companies understanding of a product or service and when an interactive experience manifests such a breakdown in the information architecture, usability failures occur.

To remedy the issues that present themselves in product-led briefs information architects will endeavor to look beyond the immediate problem space presented in the channel (for example the website alone). Research will be conducted into the broader organization (through stakeholder interviews, site visits, etc.), the market place will be reviewed and understood (through competitor analysis, best practice reviews, etc.) and users will be researched (through, for example, card sorting or user interviews).

By conducting research the information architect is attempting to gain a broad view and understanding of the problem in a systemic context. In practice, it is understood that although a website is the ultimate product that will be required by a client the approach remains problem-led and furthermore that dependencies and constraints exist beyond the product (from within the organization, in the market context and in the lives of users). In this sense, the information architect is tacitly acknowledging the presence of a problem/solution ecology that is complex and exists in social reality.

Buchanan notes that when indeterminate problems present themselves they do so as a struggle to determine where a problem-centre lies (1992). As previously described, in attempting to understand the larger context in which the immediate problem presents itself, in the case of indeterminate problems, the identified problem can often be a symptom rather than the cause of problem itself. For example, the failure of a website to assist users in finding something may be because of differing understandings and associated language used within an organization, in the marketplace and that commonly used or expected by users.

The research required to illuminate the problem ecology thus produces very large amounts of information in addition to the information presented as the problem (for example, the information on the website itself, the structure of which may be the immediate problem).

Analysis of the indeterminate problem-in-context falls short of providing a solution however. This is because the problem manifests and means different things to different stakeholders and participants in the ecology. At best analysis can explain these views and document their inter-relationship as it presents itself on the surface, however determining a solution that resolves them requires, as we will discuss in the next section, synthetic thinking on the part of the information architect.

2.7   Ideation in Information Architecture

The objective of ideation for the information architect is the reformulation of information such that it accounts for the multiple realities of stakeholders, users and context to solve the problem/s at hand (Fenn and Hobbs 2012).

New groupings of information and relationships between these groups are created such that new structures emerge. Many techniques are applied for this including (but not limited to): concept diagrams, content maps, models (for example relationship models), personas and scenario development, customer and user journey design and card sorting.

An example of the manner in which these techniques combine to assist the information architect in synthetically resolving the problem-ecology follows: field

Fig. 2.4 A photograph of a user organizing content and functionality in a card sorting exercise

research (both qualitative and quantitative) produces data. Key themes and require-ments can be determined from an analysis of the research as well as information about users that is also analysed to create personas, which represent key groupings of types of users. Personas may be placed in scenarios that represent the contextual factors and data derived from research and both assist in formulating the informa-tion environment required by users in the scenarios while simultaneously testing the ability of the design solution/s to answer the needs of those personas. Scenarios may then be joined up across a time-based progression in a user journey that can further resolve and test solutions and their interrelation across the macro concerns of the problem ecology. The process then continues to iterate between personas and micro and macro concerns until a workable design solution is attained (Fenn and Hobbs 2012; Fig. 2.4).

It is in this way that complexity is both discovered and understood and resolved through the application of a variety of techniques embedded in information archi-tecture practice, that explicitly assist in the cognitive processes required of a de-signer for synthetic thinking (Figs. 2.5 and 2.6).

In the paper *The Information Architecture of Transdisciplinary Design Practice: rethinking Nathan Shedroff's Continuum of Understanding* (Fenn and Hobbs 2012), these authors provided two examples of techniques, card sorting and user journeys, that can assist with synthetic thinking in information architecture practice:

> In the case of [user journeys] user and business/organizational needs, content and func-tionality are mapped into engagement or relationship models that allow problems and related data from different sources (regions within problem ecologies) to come together in models that start to provide harmonies and solutions in paradox and conflict driven ecolo-gies … card sorting, takes elements of content and functionality from the problem ecology and presents them (as keywords on library cards or post-it notes) in no particular order to

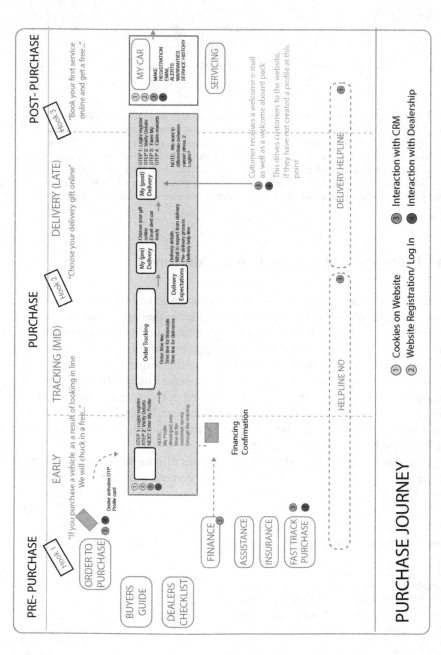

Fig. 2.5 An example of a single lifecycle stage in a user journey created for an automotive website

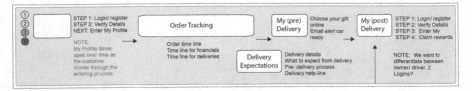

Fig. 2.6 A detail of the delivery tracking stage of the journey in Fig. 2.5

end-users of the system (where the users are representative of a cross-section of different user-types and profiles in the ecology). Users are then asked to organize (categorise or group) elements of content and functionality in ways that are meaningful to them. Through this collaborative design process information architecture designers are able to understand the conceptual-models applied by users when they interact with the system and thus synthesise solutions in a manner freed from the pre-conceptions of the inherent structures of the problem ecology held either by the designer or the internal stakeholders of the problem.

2.8   Prototyping in Information Architecture

Information architecture provides the foundational structural solution to problems, however the information architecture is often hidden in the end-product (the artifact experienced by the end-user).[5] One could say that the act of the synthetic resolution of the problem/solution ecology through the practice of information architecture provides the design solution which is distinct from the design artifact.

The information architecture is not the final, experienced artifact. In the case of a website, the graphic design, functionality and content tend to be the explicit elements that make-up the user experience: they are tacitly experienced. The underlying structure that allows all these parts to sit harmoniously (or inharmoniously) together is the information architecture.[6]

This is most clearly observed in the deliverables of information architecture. In website design site maps are used to show how content and functionality will be categorized into hierarchies that the end-user ultimately will click through (using hyperlinks), through the design of navigation and code programmed by a coder (Fig. 2.7). Task-flows reveal how pages should be linked, in which order, with what content and functionality within, so that the end-user can have an optimal experi-

---

[5] The popular community-based and practice-led website of IA "Boxes & Arrows 2014" has used the tag line 'The design behind the design' for many years.

[6] It is worth noting that the IA that exists may not ever have been explicitly designed or have been created by someone that self-identifies with the role of IA. This is often the case when an original IA design has morphed over time into something that no longer holds the original principles and objectives of the design or when a programmer, graphic designer or even project manager has been tasked with designing a website when no skilled information architect is present to contribute to the thinking.

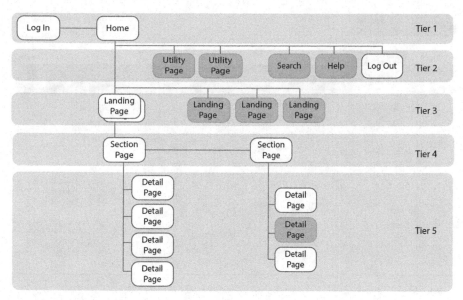

Fig. 2.7 A site map for a website. The tiers at *right* reveal how content and functionality will be displayed in navigation at different levels of the website. Note that each item of content and functionality has an associated code that references the page type and wireframe for that page

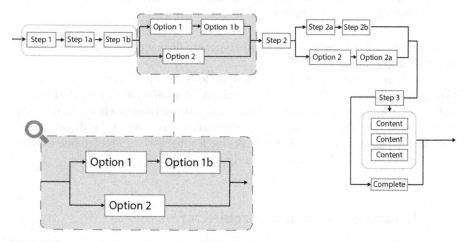

Fig. 2.8 An example of a task flow. Each block represents a page in a website (and flow)

ence in attempting to complete a task through their interaction with functionality, for example a log in process (Fig. 2.8). The information architect will also define the layout of navigation, content and functionality in pages and define different page-types that contain the rules for the display and behavior of pages at different levels of the hierarchy in a site map (Fig. 2.9) however it is the code used to build

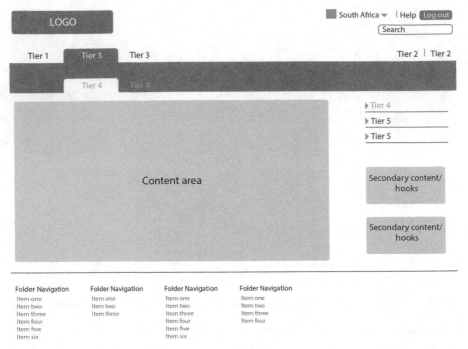

Fig. 2.9 An example of a wireframe where the aforementioned tiers in the sitemap hierarchy are being demonstrated as areas of navigation

the webpages and the graphic design and content in the pages that the end-user will directly perceive and interact with.

These three examples provide the basis for lo-fidelity prototypes, which can be tested with users even at this early stage in the development of the final design artifact. Categorizations derived from site maps can be tested with users for their ability to assist them in finding content; users can be walked through tasks; and wireframes presented to gain an understanding and receive feedback of user preference for layout, information hierarchies, styles of navigation, etc.

2.9   Reframing Information Architecture

Thus far we have explored both DT and information architecture across the stages of Research, Ideation and Prototyping and presented many respects in which these two approaches overlap. In particular information architecture presents ways of thinking, tools and techniques that assist in the organization of very large amounts of data and information that explicitly reveal the cognitive resolution of the problem/solution ecology. It is equally clear however that information architecture is at present awkwardly framed in a product-led orientation where its approach to Research, Ideation and Prototyping struggle to conform.

It is the authors' conviction that three dominant views (we call them 'illusions') held of and within the field of information architecture account for the current framing of information architecture. Through a discussion of these illusions we hope to present an alternative view, a reframing, of information architecture.

2.9.1 Illusion 1

It is an illusion drawn from the dominant view of the application of information architecture that presents the product-led deliverables of information architecture as information architecture. The activities of information architecture design, first and foremost, seek to synthetically resolve problem/solution ecologies (during Ideation) through the re-organization of data (accumulated in Research), which the deliverables of information architecture (Prototypes) strive to describe although it may not appear this way in practice since the resolution is expressed in deliverables relevant to the product-led brief, like wireframes for websites.

2.9.2 Illusion 2

It is an illusion drawn from the dominant view of the application of information architecture that its thinking, tools and techniques, overwhelmingly, serve only the information environments of the Internet and World Wide Web. All the above examples from the preceding three sections of this paper are drawn from the product-led orientation of website design, however other examples exist that assist in this repositioning of information architecture.

First, user journeys[7] have become a frequently applied tool in Service Design[8] where they offer a representation of the path a user will take through a service that can span multiple lifecycle stages (usually derived from relationship, engagement or interaction models), channels, touchpoints, content and functionality, while demonstrating related factors such as the emotional state of the user, interaction modes, key marketing messages, micro barriers and breakpoints (drop-off) along the way. Here, it is the structure of the broader service-environment that is being described through a tool that allows for the organization of multiple data sources (derived from the problem ecology) to provide a synthetic solution.

Second, in their book *Pervasive Information Architecture: Designing Cross-Channel User Experiences* (2011), Resmini and Rosati present five heuristics (Place-making, Consistency, Resilience, Reduction and Correlation) that specifi-

---

[7] Based on the professional experience of the authors, user journeys have been applied extensively in the field of information architecture design for over 13 years with specific reference to the evaluation, research and design of digital experiences (in particular website design).

[8] In the field of Service Design user journeys are referred to as Customer Journey Maps, Journey Maps or Experience Maps.

cally argue the way in which pervasive logics for the formation of structures across channels can form the basis of experiences that take their meaning, in part, through structures, that in the first instance, are not channel specific. For example, they describe Correlation as "...the capability of a pervasive information architecture model to suggest relevant connections among pieces of information, services, and goods to help users achieve explicit goals or stimulate latent needs" (Resmini and Rosati 2011). Note that there is no mention of channel or media; rather, it is correlations between the "pieces of information, services and goods" (Resmini and Rosati 2011) that ultimately are experienced across channels, or independent of any particular channel, that the information architecture seeks to design and define. Further they describe (Resmini and Rosati 2011) the way in which these heuristics operate in the context of one another:

> correlation strategies of course impact on other heuristics. Correlation helps reduce the paradox of choice (reduction [...] especially when dealing with focus and magnification), supplies alternative and custom navigation paths (resilience), and ultimately facilitates a berry-picking approach (place-making, resilience)

2.9.3   Illusion 3

It is an illusion drawn from the dominant view of the application of information architecture that it's meaning (relevance, value and purpose) is derived from its ability to deliver measurable value to businesses. Again, the activities of information architecture design, first and foremost, seek to make sense of problem/solution ecologies through the synthetic composition of data into meaningful forms. That through this process information architecture is able to deliver measurable value to businesses is a consequence of the underlying activity of information architecture design. Mistaking the one for the other, and combined with the previous illusions (that information architecture is defined by its product-led, 'digitally focused' deliverables), presents a radical misrepresentation and limitation of the meaning (relevance, value and purpose) of information architecture.

The distinction between design solution and design artifact provides the opportunity for the application of information architecture to extend beyond its current application in practice. It is in the act of synthesis that composition occurs and it is in this act of composition, that new meanings through new structural forms and arrangements of parts, is created. The cognitive resolution of the problem/solution ecology is the synthetic composition of meaning.

In *A Tale of Love and Darkness* (2005), author Amos Oz, as a young boy, has recently been granted a small space for the placement of his books alongside his father's in their personal library. The author has chosen to arrange his books by height, much to the dismay of his academically inclined father:

> At the end of the silence Father began talking, and in the space of twenty minutes he revealed to me the facts of life. He held nothing back. He initiated me into the deepest secrets of the Librarians lore: he laid bare the main highway as well as the forest tracks,

dizzying prospects of variations, nuances, fantasies, exotic avenues, daring schemes, and even eccentric whims. Books can be arranged by subject, by alphabetic order of author's names, by series or publishers, in chronological order, by languages, by topics, by areas and fields or even by place of publication. There are so many different ways

To Library Scientists and information architects reading this passage, Oz's description is a merely romantic and unspectacular look at what can be achieved when one categorizes books using their meta-data.

What is more interesting are the lines which follow immediately on from this:

And so I learnt the secret of diversity. Life is made up of different avenues. Everything can happen in one of several ways, according to different musical scores and parallel logics. Each of these parallel logics is consistent and coherent in its own terms, perfect in itself, indifferent to all the others... So I learnt from books the art of composition

Oz uses the organizing of books on a shelf as a metaphor for both the many views, understandings and choices we have and make that become our lives ("*the facts of life*"), and design or art making ("*composition*").[9]

Alternatively we can think of this as a description of one's path to the creation and discovery of ones own personal meanings, views of the world and interpretations of reality. Viewed as an act of composition, much of what we take for granted (and often as fact) that has been through a process of structuring, categorization or association, informs our understanding of the world.[10]

The process of structuring, categorizing and association (the fundamental characteristics of information architecture design in the view of the authors) is a creative one: where once a dysfunctional formation existed (multiple disparate data sources without any over-arching, coherent sense of logic, structure or harmony), the designer will have manifested structure, categorizations and associations that create new meaning (through new formal structures) for its audiences.

An example would be the choice by an information architecture of organizational schema used in the categorization of content and functionality for a website. Many schemas exist and can be used in conjunction or as hybrids however a few examples include: tasked-based, topic-based, audience-based, chronological, A–Z index, by-popularity, etc. A body of data may lend itself to one or other schema however, and very often, multiple schemas may be applicable and the choice of which to apply not only affects the ability of the end-user to complete a task but it can also change the meaning of the data for the end-user (Fig. 2.10).

---

[9] A minor edit of Oz's latter paragraph starts to read a little like a description of the way people can navigate websites and the effort that information architects take to relationally structure navigation, to hyperlink data, in ways that provide multiple options for journeying through a single structured logic of associations: "made up of different avenues (...) everything can happen in one of several ways (...) parallel logics (...) [e]ach (...) consistent and coherent in its own terms, perfect in itself, indifferent to all the others".

[10] This should not be confused with knowledge however. One simple example would be the Genus of Species: our understanding of the animal kingdom, and what it means to us, would be very different today had an alternative categorisation been applied. In Umberto Eco's "*The Name of the Rose*" the Abbott provides the categorization: celestial, terrestrial, aerial and aquatic (1980).

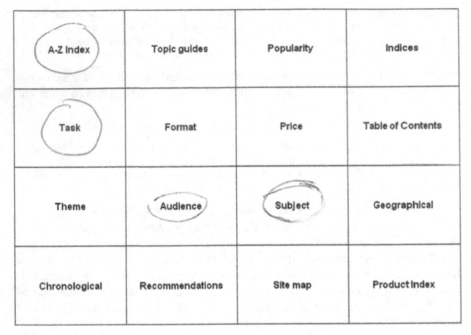

A-Z Index	Topic guides	Popularity	Indices
Task	Format	Price	Table of Contents
Theme	Audience	Subject	Geographical
Chronological	Recommendations	Site map	Product Index

Fig. 2.10 Displays a collection of 14 organizational schemas compiled by Margaret Hanley (2011) and is used in helping new comers to the field identify schemas in websites in a manner similar to playing Bingo

In the product-oriented world of website design schemas are decided upon by evaluating their ability to assist users in answering their needs (finding what they want) and those of the business (buying something, for instance) in as efficient and effective a manner as possible. The successful composition of meaning here is measured by analysis of analytics that tell us that users are quick to find what they're after and move smoothly to purchase.

However consider the example of two different ways to present the History of Art through organizing information. One uses a chronological schema and presents the History of Art from the rock paintings of Southern Africa, to Ancient Greece and Rome, all the way through to the Twentieth Century, Dada, Surrealism, Pop Art, etc. Alternatively a second schema presents artists and art works by theme: Feminism, Marxism, Post-Modernism, etc. To any student of art history these two ways of organizing and presenting information will offer very different meanings.

There are two important points to be made here. First, if the value of the field of information architecture lies first and foremost in business-relative measurability of the product-led design artifact then it hides what the authors consider the more self-evident and valuable act of indeterminate problem solving and meaning-making, even for businesses. Second, the potential relevance, value and meaning of the field of information architecture is limited, both in practice and theory, by a product-led view since in that framework Research, Ideation and Prototyping are limited by assumptions inherent in the artifactual outcome.

2.10 Conclusions

The practice of design thinking when considered foremost as a discipline neutral, people-centred, problem-solving practice has many similarities to the reframed view of information architecture as argued for in this paper. Both consider the process of problem solving as embedded within the social realities of people; both recognise that the outcome of a rich exploration of the contexts of the problem would result in vast and unresolved data, which viewed collectively results in a high level of complexity; and both consider the act of identifying and understanding the often illusive and complex problem as a fundamental step in solving the problem.

Both design thinking and information architecture recognise that the resolution of found problems, may take various forms and are unique as they are constructed in reference to the particularities of specific problem contexts. This integrated process of identifying solutions through a deeper understanding of problems and their contexts and in return understanding the problems, better, through the embedded knowledge, affordances and limitations of the solution is systemic and iterative. Just as problems are often complex with multiple solutions the act of problem resolution is also complex.

In our paper we have argued that various dominant understandings (the three illusions) derived from the product-led practice of information architecture prevalent today mask what information architecture actually does, that is, make meaning through making sense of the problem/solution ecology. Various implications for information architecture follow:

- the utility offered by the field's practices extend beyond digital products and have a broader value-proposition;
- by broadening the research frame and assumptions regarding the type of design artifacts to emerge from problem/solution conjectures, information architecture becomes a discipline, channel and artifact neutral form of problem solving;
- the field itself struggles to articulate its value; we believe that by explaining it accurately the value will present itself;
- and as in design thinking, from this position, information architecture becomes a tool for innovation.

It follows that the thinking skills, methods and techniques of information architecture would do well to be repositioned as important indeterminate problem solving tools. Further, because the structure of synthetically produced meaning formations is explicitly articulated through information architecture, the meaning (usually hidden in design artifacts) becomes available for debate at more critical, social levels.

Lastly, because the formation of meaning is explicitly articulated in information architecture, its application in design practice becomes self-reflective and self-reflective design presents bridges between practice, theory and teaching vital for preparing students of design for the ever-increasing complexity of the problems of our world.

References

Boxes & Arrows. (2014) http://www.boxesandarrows.com. Accessed 12 Jan 2014.
Brown, T. (June 2008). *Design thinking*. Harvard Business Review, pp. 84–92.
Buchanan, R. (1992). Wicked problems. *Design Issues, 8*(2), 5–21.
Cross, N. (2006). *Designerly ways of knowing*. London: Springer.
Dindler, C. (2010). The construction of fictional space in participatory design practice. *CoDesign: International Journal of CoCreation in Design and the Arts, 6*(3), 167–182.
Eco, U. (1980). *The name of the rose*. Harvest Books: San Diego.
Fenn, T., & Hobbs, J. (2012). *The information architecture of transdisciplinary design practice: Rethinking Nathan Shedroff's continuum of understanding*. In E. Appiah (Ed.), DDR 2012. 2nd International Conference on Design, Development & Research, Cape Town, South Africa.
Hanley, M. (2011). *Fill in the IA gap*. ASIS & T European Information Architecture Summit (EuroIA) 2011.
Harris, P., & Ambrose, G. (2009). *Basic design: Design thinking*. Lausanne: Ava Publishing.
Highmore, B. (2008). *The design culture reader*. London: Routledge.
Hobbs, J., Fenn, T., & Resmini, A. (2010). Maturing a practice. *Journal of Information Architecture, 2*(1), 37–54.
Koskinen, I., Zimmerman, T., Binder, J., Redstrom, S., & Wensveen, J. (Eds.) (2011). *Design research through practice: From the lab, field and practice*. San Francisco: Morgan Kaufmann.
Krippendorf, K. (2007). Design: An oxymoron? In R. Michel (Ed). *Design research now*. Basel: Birkhauser Verlag AG.
Lockwood, T. (Ed.). (2010). *Design thinking: Integrating innovation, customer experience, and brand value*. Design Management Institute.
Oz, A. (2005). *Tale of love and darkness*. London: Vintage Books.
Plomp, T., & Nieveen, N. (Eds.) (2009). *An introduction to educational design research*. Enschede: SLO—Netherlands Institute for Curriculum Development.
Resmini, A., & Rosati, L. (2011). *Pervasive information architecture—designing cross-channel user experiences*. Burlington: Morgan Kaufmann.
Rittel, H., & Webber, M. (1973). Dilemmas in a general theory of planning. *Policy Sciences, 4*, 155–169.
Van der Merwe, J. (2010). A natural death is announced. *Design Issues, 26*(3), 6–17.
Weiner, U. (2009). *Design thinking process*. HPI School of Design Thinking, Universitat Potsdam. Cape Town UX Forum Meet-Up, March 2010.
Wurman, R. S. (1997). *Information architects*. Zurich: Graphis Press.

Chapter 3
Dynamic Information Architecture—External and Internal Contexts for Reframing

Duane Degler

Abstract Professional disciplines evolve in response to a changing environment outside and inside of the discipline, in order to remain relevant and provide value to the communities they serve. This paper contributes to the conversation within the information architecture community by reflecting on some of these forces and what they may imply for the discipline as it grows. An array of external drivers for change are introduced, including the expectations of the user, evolution in data and technology, and challenges in society that could benefit from information architecture engagement. Internal drivers for change are then outlined, including the relationship between information architecture and user experience, engaging the wider stakeholder community, the practice within development methodologies, and information architecture skills. The goal is simply to introduce these forces into the discussion for consideration as part of reframing information architecture.

3.1 External and Internal Drivers

Professional disciplines evolve in response to a changing environment outside and inside of the discipline, in order to remain relevant and provide value to the communities they serve. The next evolution of information architecture (IA), like those before (Resmini and Rosati 2012), reflects the current context in which the discipline supports preserving, accessing, finding and using information to improve understanding and knowledge. The context can be better understood by reflecting on the drivers that are acting on the discipline itself.

This paper contributes to the conversation within the information architecture community by reflecting on some of the forces and what they may imply for the discipline as it grows. It is based on the author's experience of information architecture practice, as well as in his research and involvement with other organizations that have gone through these cycles of growth. For example:

D. Degler (✉)
Design for Context, Bethesda, MD, USA
e-mail: duane@designforcontext.com

A. Resmini (ed.), *Reframing Information Architecture,* Human-Computer Interaction Series,
DOI 10.1007/978-3-319-06492-5_3, © Springer International Publishing Switzerland 2014

- UXPA: The User Experience Professionals Association (formerly the Usability Professionals Association), now 22-years-old, has been through discussions about certification (2001–2002)[1], exploring a body of knowledge (2004)[2] as a mechanism to support formalization, establishment of an academic journal (the Journal of Usability Studies, 2005)[3], and most recently a reframing of identity from "usability" to "user experience" (2012).
- IEEE: The Foreword to the "SWEBOK"[4]—the Software Engineering Body of Knowledge (IEEE 2004)—describes the long evolution of formalization in the software industry, and some of the catalysts, motivations, and milestones.
- Nursing: Outside the information and design world, older established professions evolve to meet the changing needs of their constituents as well as changing understanding of themselves and their role in society (Shaw 1993).

3.1.1 External Drivers

External drivers include both social situations and technology evolutions, including the following that are discussed below:

- The emerging "Context Web" and need for dynamic information architecture;
- Evolving user expectations and blending user roles;
- Evolving data/technology environments;
- Linked data, heterogeneous data, and the Semantic Web;
- Important societal challenges.

3.1.2 Internal Drivers

Internal drivers are indicative of maturing practices, as well as the articulation among practitioners and researchers of the value systems that inform their work. The drivers that are discussed below are:

- Living in the shadow of User Experience (UX);
- Interacting with different IT/information development processes;
- Learning the skills of an Information Architect.

3.2 Why Consider both Internal and External Drivers

It is useful to gather perspectives on both the external and internal drivers for change, as it helps us understand the relevance and priorities of new ideas.

---

[1] http://www.upassoc.org/upa_projects/body_of_knowledge/certification_project.

[2] http://usabilitybok.org/usability-bok-history.

[3] https://uxpa.org/publication/journal-usability-studies.

[4] http://www.computer.org/portal/web/swebok.

External drivers help us understand "fit" and motivation—they establish the perceived relevance of our profession to those who consume our work (whether services, products, or research), and thus establish our profession as viable to others' needs. The external drivers also provide a large portion of the motivation for people who want to join the profession—they seek approaches that will help them address challenges or take advantage of opportunities they see in the world around them. What they expect from the information architecture discipline is to enhance their capability to fit with external needs and opportunities.

Internal drivers reflect maturity and evolution among the discipline's practitioners, and the goal of solidifying foundations. It may be useful to think about the evolution of a profession's development as a series of stages:

1. Emergence: A mixture of synthesis and divergence from existing disciplines. Early practitioners aim to articulate the unique attributes of the discipline.
2. Experimentation: Refining and sharing methods that form the basis of the practice. This consensus building draws more people into the discipline.
3. Codifying: With growing norms, there is increasing internal motivation to formalize and provide theoretical foundations to pass down to new members of the community and use as a way of establishing qualitative measures.
4. Maturity: There is broad understanding of the nature and role of the discipline, as well as formal established practices. Leaders in the discipline can become both guardians of it and also catalysts for change that help it adjust to changing external contexts.

It is important to consider external and internal drivers in conjunction with each other, because they are not always in harmony in their direction, creating a tension in the community. Within information architecture, the external drivers are influenced by rapid evolution, a focus on social and subjective structures, increasingly diverse contexts, integration across platforms and information sources, dynamic data relationships, and increasing automation under-the-covers of our interactions. Internal drivers are influenced by needs for more formalized, sustainable frameworks for both educating information architects and carrying out day-to-day practice. At the same time, internal and external drivers call for the discipline to be responsive to changing contexts.

3.3 External Drivers for Reframing

The Internet, as an enabling network and distributed repository, is rapidly evolving out of Web 2.0 in ways that do not fit a linear label like "Web 3.0," because the changes are happening broadly and unevenly on many fronts. Our relationship with the loose, interconnected information/communication space will appear very different in 5–10 years. The current evolution is toward a Context Web where the delivery, presentation, and inter-relating of information must be responsive to a range of attributes[5].

---

[5] The impact of context on the evolution of information architecture has been articulated by a number of people, see for example Hinton (2010).

What are the attributes that influence the user's experience, and set the context for finding, understanding and using information? The Context Web is:

- Relevant;
- Integrated;
- Illuminating;
- Interactive;
- Personal;
- Social;
- Mobile;
- Location-aware;
- Situated;
- Ambient;
- Temporal;
- Multi-modal.

As we reflect on the implications of the above list, one implication stands out: *We cannot control all these attributes in a static, deliberately designed manner*. The perception of information architecture as a structural, organizing discipline is not the only information architecture of the future. The information architecture discipline that has begun to emerge as a result is a *Dynamic information architecture*.

For the purposes of exploring the contextual drivers for reframing, here is a working definition:

> Dynamic information architecture helps provide a coherent framework for a user's experience, allowing many contextual forces to interact with each other in a way that is transparent, yet able to be controlled by the user.

Dynamic information architecture is at the heart of my information architecture practice, in order to address information environments such as:

- Publishing, where repositories routinely hold hundreds of thousands or many millions of large documents. The information architecture has to incorporate: task-specific use on different platforms; different technical formats such as ePub and highly interactive HTML; navigable visualizations and pattern-representations of large content sets; granular interactions with chunks of content rather than entire documents, where each chunk must be characterized for application control; related linking information models that reflect the user context, evolving nature of a subject domain, evolving available content from multiple sources, and user tasks/intentions.
- Highly personalized mobile applications, where local and subject recommendations are based on algorithmic agents that work with a large number of user, location, and content signals to synthesize a large amount of information and deliver it in small, relevant packages. Since "relevance" can be highly situational and subjective, user control is a key design principle.
- Collaborative and transactional workflow applications, where users carry out complex tasks and have very situational information needs. The goal is to effectively structure tasks and to deliver information *proactively* to support user

tasks, rather than assuming that users will interrupt their thought processes to seek information.

- Digital humanities, sometimes described now as "GLAM" (Galleries, Libraries, Archives and Museums). These projects are characterized by the need for information integrity over very long timescales, huge volumes of information, significant actions taken on individual artifacts (such as digitizing an ancient scroll or restoring a famous painting—which require detailed information capture and sharing), and rich information integration/evolution. These communities have been actively moving toward linked open data[6] as a way of supporting information sharing and evolution while maintaining metadata integrity.

While some of the above examples may not be the norm among information architecture projects across the community, I believe they are increasingly going to become the norm as the drivers described below influence information architecture practice.

3.4 Evolving User Expectations and Blending User Roles

Over-arching user expectations have not changed much over the years: Support my ability to achieve my real-world goals, empower me in my use of technology, and do not make the experience too hard or frustrating.

What has changed over the years is the way that this is manifest in the tools used: Anticipate my spatial/temporal/device context, respond rapidly to my diverse information needs, provide a more noise-free relevant search experience, and weave multiple strands of information content and social relationships.

To respond to these user expectations, the underlying architecture of the information and interactions needs to be more context-aware, more goal-aware, and as a result more adaptive—that is, dynamic—to provide the appropriate balance of ease of use and richness/complexity.

People used to be primarily information consumers online. Increasingly, there is a blending of roles from: Consumer > Curator (maintaining, correcting, enhancing) > Creator (authoring, posting, sharing) > Collaborator (co-creating, iterating, discussing, negotiating) (Fig. 3.1).

Supporting the seamless movement between the roles within the user experience is an important aspect of design. The role of information architecture in design is important to keep users grounded in their activities and responsibilities, oriented to the impact of changes on the information space, as well as to define how the user's inputs are captured in ways that can be used by an application and by other users.

We must consider how we deliberately build in these roles when creating information spaces, because these roles allow more human-centered and ongoing refinement of:

---

[6] For information on the "LOD-LAM" community, see http://lodlam.net.

Fig. 3.1 Relationships
between user roles in content
environments. (Degler and
Phua 2011)

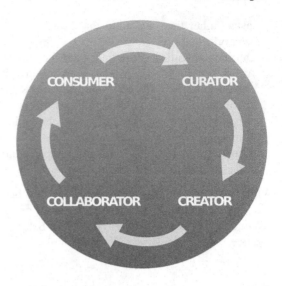

- The meaning of information—and relationships between information—as it evolves over time.
- The pruning of information and relationships as meaning changes; for example where information may be superseded by new perspectives or findings.
- New navigational mechanisms and expressions to be applied against a growing scale of information, where the volume of information leads to the need for curation of patterns (both human and algorithmic) to interpret the breadth of the information available.
- Sharing of information in environments where relevance changes over time, so what is shared before may not be a viable pattern for what is shared later.

3.5 Evolving Data and Technology Environments

There are a number of factors that influence the evolving data landscape, and touch on the role of information architecture as a core practice in future developments.

3.5.1 Intertwingularity

As described by Ted Nelson (1974, elaborated 1987), there is a movement toward a more fluid, inter-related interaction with information—networked architectures for information and for people. Nelson (1987) wrote:

> Hierarchical and sequential structures, especially popular since Gutenberg, are usually forced and artificial. Intertwingularity is not generally acknowledged—people keep pretending they can make things hierarchical, categorizable and sequential when they can't.

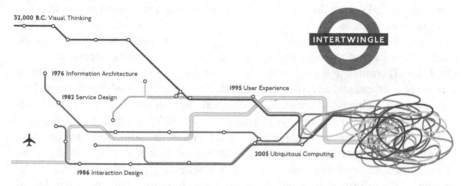

Fig. 3.2 Morville's illustration of disciplines within the "intertwingularity" (a play on the notion of the "singularity"; http://www.flickr.com/photos/morville/4530553981/in/set-72157623756701459/)

In the context of user experience and information architecture, Peter Morville described this trend in *Ambient Findability* (2005) and then represented it as a convergence of disciplines in 2010 (Fig. 3.2).

The combination of cross-linking, categorization, and user tagging can, in deeply intertwingled information environments, lead to "anything from anywhere" problems, where every avenue used to find something leads to virtually every item of information in the collection—making the entire collection unbounded and therefore meaningless. Information scientists are working on algorithms and models for bounding a network in ways that identify patterns of information. The tuning of these algorithms and incorporation into the user's experience are important activities for the information architecture discipline.

3.5.2 Structured Data

We see evidence of increasingly structured data all around us. One major example is the continuing stream of changes to Google's search application and incorporating the Knowledge Graph[7]—incorporating structured data from the Freebase database and other sources. The Knowledge Graph appears most visibly in Google's search suggestions and the profile cards that appear on the right side of the page if you have searched for a common "entity" (for example, "Nelson Mandela" or "Eiffel Tower").

It keys off of known entities that have detailed and reliable data in Freebase, traversing the available structure to provide profile data and also relationships to other entities that might be of interest to the user. One goal is to provide an answer to a factual question without requiring the user to leave the search results page. When

---

[7] For an overview of Knowledge Graph, see http://www.google.com/insidesearch/features/search/knowledge.html. For developer information, see https://developers.google.com/freebase/.

people select links from the profile, it also provides input to underlying search and advertising algorithms.

Facebook is increasingly leveraging the Open Graph[8] structure, which uses the relationships between people and topics (music, film, interests, locations, etc.— which are all entities to the system) to create underlying models of interests that it uses to recommend and advertise. Because the Open Graph capability is embedded in many other web sites, it means Facebook and the data network also has connections with many non-Facebook web pages where the sharing module is embedded.

These uses of structured data, among many others, by large hub sites provides a significant amount of encouragement to the web development community to increase embedded page data structure, including scheme.org markup, RDFa, etc. So the role of the information architecture extends to how meaning and relationships are encoded in page markup, and what effect that has on information's wider role on the Web.

Within the IT architecture community, techniques such as Domain-Driven Design (Evans 2002) are coming back into wider use. While there is often cynicism of the semantic web from within the information architecture community, one of the cornerstones of those data model/syntax standards is shifting the emphasis from individual data instances to the relationships that are embodied, and doing so in a way that is shareable across different applications and domains. Thus, the relationships become dynamic, evolving, with information behaving as a dispersed network graph. This has implications for how information architects should consider their "structures" as growing, evolving, and shared.

3.6   The Relationship with Data Architects and the Tech Community

While not broadly indicative, the following story is an interesting insight into information architecture's role, presence, and how we may be seen in the wider community. On April 27, 2012, a question was posed on the Semantic Arts blog[9]. The question came from Dave McComb, President of Semantic Arts, a leading practitioner and trainer in areas of enterprise data modeling, ontology/taxonomy modeling, and semantic technology applications. The question was not widely disseminated or particularly notable in itself, but perhaps is one of those "canaries in the coal mine" regarding our external relationship with data technologists. Dave wrote:

> When did the term Information Architect become associated with web navigational design? This one sort of snuck up on us. I'm thinking it happened in the last 2–4 years. The term wasn't in wide use prior to that, but prior to that people would have assumed that is had to do with data modeling or something. Now it is a sub discipline of web site usability and setting up taxonomies [sic] that enable better user navigation. [10]

---

[8] For an Open Graph overview, see https://developers.facebook.com/docs/opengraph/overview/.

[9] Semantic Arts, http://semanticarts.com/.

[10] http://web.archive.org/web/20120620061118/http://www.semanticarts.com/engage/discuss-0/bid/135237/when-did-the-term-information-architect-become-associated-with-web-navigational-design. Not currently available anymore at the original location. Accessed January 2014.

Fortunately, this specific post was rapidly commented by key people in the information architecture community offering clarification and outreach. But it is an interesting reflection on the awareness gap between information architecture and practicing data/enterprise architects. Some of us walk freely between those worlds—and I have heard this kind of misconception from many systems architects, data modelers and developers. As a discipline, information architecture may currently be perceived as "a sub-discipline of web site usability and setting up taxonomies [sic] that enable better user navigation" (and among ourselves, user experience—more below). This is problematic if our discipline aims to influence the deeper aspects of the technology landscape and engage in the more dynamic data and metadata capabilities that increasingly drive web and mobile design.

In my experience, the IT data and enterprise architecture communities are very open to involvement and collaboration. For me, this happens in projects by organizing early ideation and information sharing activities, to identify technical implications behind information design and build a common language with other architects. At a broader professional level, in order to engage credibly with these communities, I spend time in their communities by attending conferences and meetings where they explore key issues in technology development. This helps me understand the underlying vehicles upon which information is carried and also builds important personal relationships. One other thing that helps build bridges is to have insights into the touch-points between the various disciplines, by identifying where information architecture practices intersect or fill gaps in other technology practices and processes. So we can become familiar with reference standards such as the SWEBOK (Software Engineering Body of Knowledge, published by IEEE)[11], the EABOK (Enterprise Architecture Body of Knowledge)[12] and even the PMBOK (Project Management Body of Knowledge)[13], each of which outline the core attributes in the disciplines. This work is similar to what the information architecture community is doing when exploring its role within user experience.

3.6.1 Linked Data, Heterogeneous Information, and the Semantic Web

"Big data" currently has much of the attention in the press and the technology community. While big data currently has the focus of popular attention, the potentially more transformational movement driving long-term information architecture is happening with *linked data*, driven in part by governments, foundations and corporations actively participating in providing *open* linked data.

Linked data aims to break down silos of information, but at the same time this means that the data users interact with may no longer be from only one source. For designers, the data used in applications is thus not as predictable, manually crafted, or controllable—yet it is more highly structured and provides richer opportunities

---

[11] SWEBOK, http://www.computer.org/portal/web/swebok.

[12] EABOK, http://www2.mitre.org/public/eabok/.

[13] PMBOK, http://www.pmi.org/PMBOK-Guide-and-Standards.aspx.

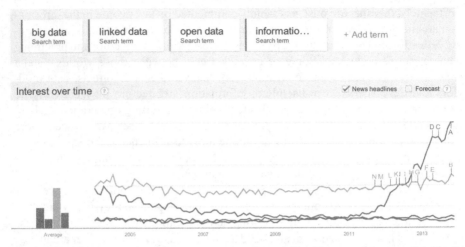

Fig. 3.3 Snapshot from Google Trends illustrating the news headline use of the term "big data" as compared to other information architecture and data relevant terms. (http://www.google. com/trends/explore#q=big+data,linked+data,open+data,information+architecture&hl=en-US. Accessed Nov 2013)

for information architecture when designing information exploration and discovery capabilities. Network models of information are becoming more prevalent than hierarchical/static models of information. IT infrastructures now focus on providing a fabric for more flexible, integrated, shared data. The information architecture discipline needs to engage and leverage this fabric (Fig. 3.3).

One of the fundamental aspects of the increase in structured, linked, and open data is that design needs to focus more heavily on data patterns and abstractions, because the volume of information and its dynamic nature can overwhelm a user's ability to comfortably focus on specific instances, as well as challenge designers and information architects to effectively model application behavior. Designs also need to reflect the encoded meanings articulated within the semantic relationships. This is strongly in the domain of information architecture, but requires consideration of how our analysis and design methods should evolve in response to changes in the data environment.

3.6.2 Heterogeneous Information

Underlying information frameworks are improving and are more easily able to share contextualizing data across application boundaries—what Thomas Vander Wal refers to as the "come to me web" (Vander Wal 2006). Examples of this include web services such as If This Then That[14], and mobile applications like Tempo and Donna[15].

---

[14] If This Then That, https://ifttt.com.

[15] Tempo, www.tempo.ai. Donna, http://don.na.

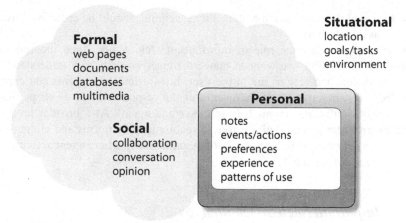

Fig. 3.4 Categories of heterogeneous information that could be enabled by a common semantic data syntax to support user interface responsiveness

The heterogeneous integration of data across applications can be represented as primarily spanning four major types of information: Formal, Social, Personal and Situational, as articulated in a CHI 2008 workshop that explored elements of semantic web data frameworks and approaches that had specific user interface impacts (schraefel et al. 2008; Fig. 3.4):

The four categories—formal, social, personal, situational—align with the attributes of the Context Web itemized previously, and can help us think about aspects of data that need to be considered as part of creating future information architectures. Two attributes of data[16] that this workshop considered important to call out may also be useful in the reframing of information architecture:

- *Seamless:* User goals and tasks are facilitated more easily, no matter what technologies and applications involved.
- *Frictionless:* Data is free to move between applications and uses as needed.

3.6.3 Agents

At the same time that the data landscape is changing, so is the enabling capability that comes from automated agents and ambient background services. One of the critical implications for information architecture practitioners, and user experience practitioners more generally, is how to help people instruct, monitor, constrain, and guide the activities of semi-autonomous and autonomous agents. These are real issues today, as agents are actively operating in the world in recommender systems, medical decision-support systems, search systems, and advertising algorithms, just to name a few. Issues of transparency, auditability, privacy and policy are coming

---

[16] For more on this concept and the discussion captured at the ASIS&T Information Architecture Summit 2011, see the workshop slides from IA 2.0: An open conversation about context, mobility and semantics at http://www.designforcontext.com/files/dd_IA-20_IASummit_20110402.pdf.

to the fore, and the information architecture discipline should be an active force in discussions and designs.

In order to consider the role of information architecture when incorporating agents into application, we want to concern ourselves with how understandable agent parameters and actions are to the user, how articulately agents can express what decisions they require of the user, and the responsibilities of all parties in the "conversation" (interactions between user and agent). At a broader level, information architecture could play a role in recommending norms and etiquettes to increase consistency and reduce user burden, particularly where agent activities are more ambient or ubiquitous.

3.6.4   Important Societal Challenges

A key driver for reframing information architecture should be the impact that the discipline has on society and the challenges we all face, whether those challenges relate to interacting with technology directly, or solutions are better enabled by technology. As a catalyst for that conversation, here are a few challenges that could help frame areas of focus for information architecture:

- Social improvement
  - Enabling access: Providing broad-based and appropriate access for people's information requirements; considering the methods of access (e.g. mobile in many parts of the world, shared devices within rural communities, etc.); sustainability of access in changing circumstances.
  - Medical information access and use: Supporting a shift from intervention to prevention; accommodating the challenge of low literacy in populations with higher medical needs; understanding the information-gathering changes arising from the "quantified self" movement, patient-centered medicine, "health 2.0" and social information sharing among patients.
  - Education and literacy: The movement in the US toward online or blended education; MOOCS (massive open online courses); educational performance and assessing quality; cross-cultural education; providing education opportunities to rural communities in many languages.
  - Environmental sustainability: Modeling and representing the system effects of our lifestyles and products; providing information that helps individuals and groups understand the impact of their actions and choices; communicating the latest research and information, and helping people understand where new information has superseded older information.
- Personal and community welfare
  - Disaster response and recovery: Managing the increasing information integration from diverse sources at point of need; harmonizing different roles and communication protocols among responders; incorporating the social and real-time mobile information streams into response management; multi-channel and cross-channel communication through public media/internet channels; layering visualization and information for augmented presentation.

- Missing persons tracking: Providing common sites for collecting and managing information (addressing the current plethora of disaster-specific sites); merging and referencing diverse information sources; disambiguation; status management, provenance, and retraction; long-term archiving of data for use by responsible organizations and researchers.
- Collective understanding
  - Managing file proliferation: Addressing the rapid expansion of stored data; increasing usefulness as scale of personal and community materials increases; extending search capabilities beyond keyword-focused search to more meaning-driven search.
  - Preservation and archiving: Assessing archival significance of "born digital" information; increasing findability of deep data; version management and online persistence; format preservation of both data and metadata; enhancing the relevance of information, particularly as it is reinterpreted and extended over time.
  - Cultural awareness: Creating digital surrogate experiences for fragile physical heritage sites; broadening cultural awareness across ever-wider populations; supporting the increasingly multi-lingual nature of the web; maintaining cultural integrity while also sharing cross-cultural collaborations.

3.7 Internal Drivers for Reframing

As part of an active user experience community in a major city, I routinely interact with a wide range of practitioners. The cross-fertilization that arises from being part of the "umbrella" of user experience enriches all our practice areas. At the same time, with breadth can come a thinning of depth. I notice that specific methods and professional awareness can be missing from others' repertoire.

As part of a project for the User Experience Professionals Association, we elaborated the following inventory of disciplines allied under the user experience umbrella (Battle and Degler 2010; Fig. 3.5).

What are the implications of a consolidation of information architecture and user experience?

- *Benefit:* Residing under a common umbrella, incorporating information architecture helps with client recognition of the important role we can play improving the information experience, and potentially reduces role-limiting for some practitioners.
- *Risk:* As marketing people say, *diluting the brand*, because a wide array of skill areas and capability levels are now homogenized into a single category. This creates confusion among potential clients, and also potentially puts downward pressure on compensation if we appear to be competing on a level playing field with people who do not bring the same toolkit to the job.

The driver for reframing is knowing the role of information architecture under the user experience umbrella. Ideally, information architecture can incorporate a user

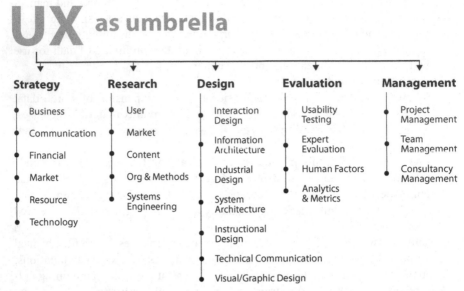

Fig. 3.5 User experience categorization scheme established for cross-discipline methods tagging, part of the UXPA *Usability Body of Knowledge* project, 2006. (http://www.usabilitybok.org; used for facets and content management)

experience perspective as a way of strengthening the awareness of clients, teams and practitioners as to the role of the user in our work—and then to use that entrée to understand deeper needs. If those deeper needs align with the specific skills of information architecture, then encourage the fit. If not, then encourage collaboration with associated peers/disciplines to achieve effective outcomes.

3.8 Interactions with IS/Information Development Processes

The practice of information architecture has always integrated itself into the larger scheme of information management and software development. Over the past ten years, we have had to consider the impact of practicing information architecture as a thoughtful, exploratory discipline within the constraints of Agile, Lean, and other development methodologies.

One implication of working within these methodologies is that they have, for the most part, been created as development methodologies. Their iterative nature, while valuable in gaining rapid feedback that is incorporated back into development, does not always easily accommodate the deep immersion into content and user needs that is required in information architecture. The analytical nature of rich content and structural modeling may not always be rapidly iterative or lightweight.

This challenge is shared by other disciplines that participate in the early foundation-setting and needs analysis of applications and systems. Systems architects, data analysts, user researchers, and designers are all working within the same evolution of their methods and techniques, and we can all learn from each other as these development methodologies evolve.

3.9 Learning the Skills of An Information Architect

What does it mean to grow and hone our skills? These skills may be core skills or they may be associated skills encompassed under user experience generally.

If you are not surrounded by other information architects (which is common in many teams or projects), how is it possible to deepen skills, learn as an apprentice, and share knowledge with others? The diffusion and virtualization of the community is a fact of life, but it is a challenge. Formal learning and publication are only one part of the picture—another part is the informal and empathetic learning that comes from shared practice and direct experience. What is the information architecture community's role?

3.10 Conclusions

There are many external and internal drivers that influence the future direction of information architecture as both a discipline and professional practice. I provided a possible perspective to support this conversation further: other valuable internal and external relationships between information architecture and other fields and disciplines can be identified which are not touched upon here, some of them being well understood parts of the ongoing work of the Information Architecture Institute (Information Architecture Institute 2011a).

So what might it mean to practice "dynamic information architecture"? That question has been important for me to consider as the information architecture community discusses the *reframing of information architecture*, and answers will evolve over time as the external environment in which information architecture contributes evolves. As a summary to my contribution above, the following is a set of challenges that could be valuable for the information architecture community to investigate further. How do we as practitioners and researchers:

- Understand the information/data/user/context ecosystem?
- Refine methods focused on networked information, user context and relevance-awareness?
- Interpret information "behaviors" and provide the appropriate level of control to encourage greater understanding?

- Engage with richer analytical/technical tools that can help understand and provide user control for increasingly complex information environments and contexts of use?
- Design for more dynamic experiences? These include: flexible and fluid interactions; platform independence and integration; knowledge of users and their patterns of use; models that represent data domains and multi-dimensional information; adaptive interactions that respond to context and perceptions of relevance.

References

Battle, L., & Degler, D. (2010). Usability knowledge online: Discover the BoK. Usability Professionals Association Conference Munich 2010. http://www.designforcontext.com/files/usabilitybok_degler-battle_2010-05-26.pdf. Accessed 20 Jun 2014.

Degler, D., & Phua, J. (2011). Lemonade out of lemons: Design increases your data's value to your users. Semantic Technologies East 2011. http://www.designforcontext.com/files/jp_dd_SemtechEAST_20111201.pdf. Accessed 17 Jan 2014.

Evans, E. (2002). *Domain-driven design: Tackling complexity in the heart of software.* Boston: Addison-Wesley Longman.

Hinton, A. (2010). The machineries of context: New architectures for a new dimension. *Journal of Information Architecture, 1*(1), 37–47. (http://journalofia.org/volume1/issue1/04-hinton/jofia-0101-04-hinton.pdf).

IEEE Computer Society. (2004). Guide to the software engineering body of knowledge (SWEBOK®). A. Abran, J. W. Moore, P. Bourque, & R. Dupuis (Eds.). http://www.computer.org/portal/web/swebok. Accessed 27 Dec 2013.

Information Architecture Institute. (2011a). The information architecture institute framework. http://iainstitute.org/en/about/. Accessed 28 Nov 2013.

Information Architecture Institute. (2011b). Meeting minutes April 2 2011. http://www.iainstitute.org/minutes/annual-members-meeting-denver-april-2-2011. Accessed 28 Nov 2013.

Morville, P. (2005). *Ambient findability.* Sevastopol: O'Reilly Media.

Nelson, T. (1974). *Computer lib/dream machines* (Rev. Ed.). Redmond: Tempus Books of Microsoft.

Resmini, A., & Rosati, L. (2012). A brief history of information architecture. *Journal of Information Architecture, 3*(2), 33–46. (http://journalofia.org/volume3/issue2/03-resmini/).

schraefel, m. c., Golbeck, J., Degler, D., Bernstein, A., & Rutledge, L. (2008). *Semantic web user interactions: Exploring HCI challenges.* In CHI '08 Extended Abstracts on Human Factors in Computing Systems (CHI EA '08). ACM.

Shaw, M. C. (1993). The discipline of nursing: Historical roots, current perspectives, future directions. *Journal of Advanced Nursing, 18*(10), 1651–1656. (http://onlinelibrary.wiley.com/doi/10.1046/j.1365-2648.1993.18101651.x/abstract). Accessed 27 Dec 2013.

Vander Wal, T. (2006). The come to me web. http://www.personalinfocloud.com/blog/2006/1/19/the-come-to-me-web.html. Accessed 17 Jan 2014.

Chapter 4
The Interplay of the Information Disciplines and Information Architecture

Sally Burford

Abstract This chapter considers the findings of studies of the situated practice of Web information architecture (IA) in organizations of varying size. The focus is on the work of web information architecture, with the aim of developing a deeper understanding of the practice and its influences. From the examination of the practice that surrounds the creation of an information-rich website, this chapter reports the disciplinary profiles of the practitioners of web information architecture and reveals the extent of the influence of the information tradition and discipline. It invites reflection on the consequences of these findings for future theory and a disciplinary base for information architecture.

4.1 Introduction

In its attention to self-definition, theory, methodology, evolution, research and conferencing, information architecture has been influenced to a large extent by the theoretical traditions and methods of the information discipline. Resmini and Rosati (2011a, p. 38) chart the history of information architecture and note the pre-web era of information architecture that focused on information systems. At this time, information architecture was concerned with structuring, modelling and diagramming of data and its interrelationships in the construction of information systems (Stair and Reynolds 2008) and its emphasis was on managing enterprise information as a resource (Evernden and Evernden 2003). Enterprise information architecture describes the process and the outcome of the high-level mapping of the total information and data holdings of an organization.

Information architecture then responded to the phenomenon of the web, developing a new identity; that of web information architecture or what is now deemed to be *classic* information architecture. Rosenfeld and Morville (1998) introduced a widely adopted theoretically-driven methodology for developing the information structures of the websites of large organization. The influence of the library and information science (LIS) discipline was significant. "The Rosenfeld and Morville

S. Burford (✉)
University of Canberra, Canberra, Australia
e-mail: sally.burford@canberra.edu.au

A. Resmini (ed.), *Reframing Information Architecture,* Human-Computer Interaction Series,   47
DOI 10.1007/978-3-319-06492-5_4, © Springer International Publishing Switzerland 2014

text was aimed at, in its own words, 'applying the principles of architecture and library science to website design'" (Dillon and Turnbull 2005, p. 1).

Throughout the era of classic information architecture and still today, scholars and practitioners of information architecture note the need for information architecture to be distinguished from pre-existing information traditions. Dillon (2001, p. 29) claimed that "the biggest obstacle to information architecture becoming a distinct discipline remains its lack of unique methods and theories". The intervening years have not seen a solution and in 2013, Davis continues to call for theory to support the practice of information architecture (Davis 2013). Furthermore, Resmini and Rosati (2011b) shift information architecture into new territory, where information is architected across contexts and channels to create integrated and meaningful information strata.

This chapter contributes to the research and knowledge base necessary for information architecture to build a disciplinary identity. It describes an examination of specific practice of web information architecture in organizational settings and exposes the subtleties and the disciplinary influences that underpin and impact the practice. In turn, these subtleties and influences can be used to build unique methods and theories for information architecture.

4.2   The Literature

Rosenfeld and Morville's (1998) seminal methodological approach to the practice of web information architecture came from a LIS tradition. This is recognised by Morville (2004, p. xiii) himself: "We became evangelists of the LIS school of information architecture. We argued passionately for the value of applying traditional LIS skills in the design of websites and intranets". Mahon and Gilchrist (2004, p. xviii) also embrace the usefulness of LIS traditions and skill sets for information architecture, saying:

> (w)e have always tended to take the LIS view—even before we began to look at information architecture, in dealing with the management issues arising as a consequence of the widespread introduction of IT and associated networking in organizations. That is not to say we have always felt that LIS had all the answers but there were, and are, skill sets in LIS that lend themselves efficiently to information architecture.

Dillon and Turnbull (2005, p. 2) note that "IA is an interdisciplinary field of practice and research" that borrows heavily from other fields of expertise including "library and information scientists who have long dealt with classification and categorization of recorded knowledge". In describing his early attempts to organise information on the internet, Rosenfeld in an interview with Carliner (2008, p. 102) reports:

> I was convinced that the detritus of the information explosion would require structure, organization, and labeling to provide any real value to users. I knew that the principles of librarianship, if ported to non-library settings, could at least partially meet this challenge.

A structured methodology and a project approach to web information architecture were proposed by Rosenfeld and Morville (1998). In this, significant influences from the information systems discipline are apparent. The traditional structured methodology or "waterfall" approach (Laudon and Laudon 2006, p. 534) prescribes the stages and tasks of an information system development in an ordered and sequenced manner. Rosenfeld and Morville's (2006, p. 231) "structured development process" for web information architecture in large organizations bears strong resemblance to the traditional, structured, *waterfall* approach to information systems development (Laudon and Laudon 2006).

Whilst the information traditions of information systems and LIS have informed the practice of information architecture, they remain disciplines and professions distinct from the realities of structuring information on corporate websites. Providing and structuring web information is relatively new in organizations and many individuals contribute to its creation and ongoing existence (Morrogh 2002). Rosenfeld and Morville (2006, p. 24) report that the web is composed of "rich streams of information flowing within and beyond the borders of departments, business units, institutions, and countries".

Burford (2011) examines the context for web information architecture practice in large organizations and exposes the difference between web information architecture and prior information traditions. Using complexity theory, she claims that the metaphor of complex adaptive system "allows the practice to be seen as emergent and self-organising, and distinguishes this instance of information organization from those that are more ordered and finite in nature" (p. 2036). Burford (2011) claims that an orderly, structured methodology conducted as project, is not an adequate instruction for the practice in large organizations and that the influences of dominant and traditional information disciplines should be challenged.

Leaving the influence of LIS traditions behind, Resmini and Rosati (2011b) highlight a new era in information architecture that acknowledges a cross-channel context for information and its user. The multiple and mobile channels of web, tablet devices, smart phones, print and physical spaces invite an information architect to take responsibility for a pervasive information layer that binds all channels in an architecture of meaning (Resmini and Rosati 2011b). With this conception of practice, a new wave of disciplinary and theoretical instability confronts information architecture. The domain is less determinable as it shifts to include a suite of varied, yet purposely-integrated information platforms.

Hobbs et al. (2010) position information architecture as having multi-disciplinary influences and include visual arts, graphic design, library science, architecture, psychology and marketing as some of the disciplines that have had theoretical and practical input to the practice and knowledge base of information architecture. Hobbs et al. (2010, p. 43) describe information architecture as a "casual practice", one without the framework of a formal institutional discipline. Practices that are grounded in an institutional discipline are benefited by a theoretical focus, an academic rigour and a high-quality, scholarly literature base. According to Hobbs et al. (2010, p. 37), information architecture does not reap these benefits and is limited by an "abundance of know-how and opinion".

Scholars have also wrestled to define information architecture. White (2004, p. 219) has the opinion that "there is no accepted definition of information architecture, and that is a good thing at this stage of its development". He draws parallels with the term *information science,* which dates from the mid-1950s and still has no agreed definition in the wider community. Resmini et al. (2009, para. 16) agree, saying "the information architecture community does not have to agree on a definition because there is more to do". Despite the difficulty and dubious wisdom in attempting to define information architecture, Resmini et al. (2009) note that many have tried over a ten year period. The unending debates and varied perspectives are due to the youthfulness of the discipline (Resmini et al. 2009, para. 6).

As many before them (Madsen 2009; Fast 2006), Hobbs et al. (2010) call for research to contribute to the building of a disciplinary knowledge base and the transformation of information architecture as casual practice, into information architecture as discipline-led practice. They promote practice-led research as a mode of inquiry that could contribute to this shift. Practice-led research positions the outcome or artefact of design work as a site of informal codification of the practice knowledge. The artefact is the starting point for reflection and interpretation of the rules, processes and conventions that were used in its creation (Hobbs et al. 2010, p.49).

Whilst research-led practice will indeed contribute to a mature discipline of information architecture, other research approaches are required. This chapter describes one such alternative approach to theorising the practice and building validated knowledge and well-rounded perspectives of information architecture. The account is of a study of socially situated practice in which the researcher is remote from the practice. Discrete websites representing the enterprise have been, and remain, an important locale for the activity of information architecture. They are the focus of this research, which steps away from the perspectives of the expert practitioner of information architecture to examine what actually happens in practice in varied organizational settings. It does not presume the presence or contribution of expertise in information architecture. It examines the reality of practice, rather than formulating or expecting method, activity or design artefact. This research attends to those who engage in the structuring of online information within situated organizational practice.

4.3 The Research Approach

For situated activity in a work and organizational context, Cook and Brown (1999, p. 386) use the term *practice,* which they define as "the coordinated activities of individuals and groups in doing their "real work" as it is informed by a particular organizational or group context". Shaw (2002, p. 119) writes of a similar understanding of practice. It is usually interpreted, she suggests, as "patterns of activity that can be mapped and grasped as wholes distinct from the persons acting in particular times and places".

Bjorkeng, Clegg and Pitsis (2009, p. 145) describe practice "as novel patterns of interaction developed into predictable arrays of activities, changing and transforming while at the same time continuing to be referred to as 'the same'". For Gherardi (2009b), practice is located in the significant pattern of how conduct or activity takes place. Objects, tools and artefacts embody knowledge and "anchor practices in their materiality" (p. 354).

> Theories of practice assume an ecological model in which agency is distributed between humans and non-humans and in which the relationality between the social world and materiality can be subjected to inquiry (Gherardi 2009b, p. 115).

Geiger (2009, p. 132) considers "practice as epistemic-normative concept". Gherardi (2006, p. 34) agrees with the notion of practice as ordering and normalising, defining practice "as a mode, relatively stable in time and socially recognised, of ordering heterogeneous items into a coherent set". She adds that practice constrains and forbids some alternatives and choices, while approving others as preferable or easier. Thus, practice becomes a normative construct where "actors share a practice if their actions are appropriately regarded as answerable to norms of correct or incorrect practice" (Rouse 2001, p. 190).

Practices are made socially recognisable or legitimised by being stabilised and institutionalised (Lawrence and Suddaby 2006; Gherardi 2009a). They stabilise to provisional agreed ways of doing things—even if that understanding is contested (Gherardi 2009a). A negotiated, shared and recognised way of working collectively means that practices shift and evolve from a relatively firm, but not fixed, foundation. In this way, the identity of both practitioners and the practice is established and can be observed from outside the practice (Gherardi 2009a, p. 356).

Research using a practice-based approach exhibits a desire "to shed new light on organizational phenomena by getting closer to the real work in organizations" and a move away from structural notions of organizations (Geiger 2009, p. 129). By locating an inquiry within a practicing community, and in focusing on the activity and subjective accounts of practitioners, "we gain a deeper understanding of how organizations are constructed, how they are changed, how innovations emerge, how decisions are made and how knowledge is generated" (Geiger 2009, p. 135). Gherardi (2009b) sees practice as a powerful concept in organizational studies because of the plurality of its semantic possibilities. "Practice is a malleable term which can be put to numerous uses and employed to denominate many aspects of the phenomenal reality under study" (Gherardi 2009b, p. 116).

It is these understandings of practice that form the foundation for the study of the practice of web information architecture in large organizations (Burford 2011, 2014) and small and medium enterprises (SMEs) (Burford and Given 2013). This examination of the practice of information architecture ignores the opinions and expertise of experienced practitioners and thought-leaders in the field and looks directly at situated organizational practice.

The research investigates the practice of structuring information on an organizational website in order that a clientele is well informed. Two separate studies that are distinguished by organizational size were conducted using similar research approaches. Burford (2011) claims that her study of the practice of web information architecture in large organizations has reached "theoretical sufficiency" (Dey 1999, p. 257), whilst the second study (Burford and Given 2013), which examines practice in SMEs is a preliminary investigation of five organizations and requires extension. All data collection took place in Australia.

Designed as a particularistic, multiple, case studies (Merriam 1998, p. 29), both research projects examined a particular phenomenon within organizational contexts. Each case was important for what it revealed about the conduct of web information architecture in the organization. Rather than describe how information architecture is practiced in any particular organization, the research was designed to find trends and patterns across practices. Eisenhardt (2007, p. 25) writes that the analysis of multiple case studies enables "recognizing patterns of relationships among constructs within and across cases and their underlying logical arguments".

Hartley (2004, p. 323) claims that "case studies can be useful for exploring new or emerging processes or behaviours" and understanding "how behaviour and/or processes are influenced by, and influence context". A case study approach to knowing more about how organizations carry out web information architecture is applicable because contextual insights and patterns will be revealed only by examining situated practice.

In both studies, organizations with websites that are publicly accessible and predominantly used to inform clients were invited to participate. Organizations were not drawn from a particular sector; rather, they were selected according to size and the presentation of a public-facing, information-rich website. To distinguish appropriately by size, SMEs were included in the study if the number of employees was less than 200. Large organizations with 300 or more employees were recruited. Leaving a gap of 100 employees between the research recruitment criteria for large organizations and SMEs was a strategy to avoid the various definitions of organizational size and to ensure that organizational sizes were well distinguished, rather than representing a continuum.

A qualitative approach to data collection was used throughout. The people with responsibility and involvement in structuring online information were recruited to tell the story of practice within the organization. The group semi-structured interviews varied in composition and size, from one to four people within the organization and included the person in the role of web manager where one existed.

For each study, the data arising from the interviews, were captured in digital audio format, and were transcribed professionally. In an inductive approach to analysis, the data were coded using NVivo as a supporting analytic tool to reveal patterns and themes across all of the studied organizations. Initial open coding was conducted in a detailed scrutiny of the data. In a process of constant comparison (Charmaz 2006) the most prominent open codes as well as higher level constructs resulting in the amalgamation of open codes were used to construct a conceptual framework of practice. This approach provided a theoretical freedom to approach a complex body of data and reveal themes and insights without pre-existing expectations or existing coding frames.

4.4   Practice in Large Organizations

The influence of prior information disciplines, particularly LIS and IS, dominates the practice of web information architecture in large organizations. Two of the seven organizations that were studied employed, full-time web information architects. Other organizations claimed that they had an adequate level of information architecture ability within the web team and that a single specialist was not required. On an occasional basis, several organizations used consultant information architects whenever the need for a greater level of expertise in information architecture was recognised. Two organizations acknowledged that web information architecture was achieved internally by central web staff with no real training or expertise, other than the knowledge that was gleaned of necessity.

Those organizations that had internal, dedicated positions in web information architecture were adamant that this was the best approach. The internal information architect would be present at all stages of the work of information architecture, especially the inevitable changes to information and its structures that in the socially complex environment of large organizations (Burford 2011). Small, ongoing, agile approaches to web information architecture could be fostered. The need for deep knowledge of the specific business context and culture and daily ongoing interactions with business stakeholders were reported as invaluable to the work of web information architecture. With unsuccessful consultant-led web information architecture projects behind him, one research participant concluded:

> And our previous experience was that when we had consultants come in, do a quick job and go, they never, they never understood the culture of the department and quite often they didn't have sufficient sector experience to understand the tensions or the subject matter, the business processes or the nature of the organization. (Org B)

Regardless of their current expertise, the practitioners of web information architecture were drawing from a practice knowledge-base grounded in information traditions and were keen to learn more to support their practice. They engaged with the extant knowledge-base in a variety of ways reporting: lots of reading, "just experience on the job—I've been through a lot of website redevelopments (Org C)", "picking up stuff from external people that we have had in (Org D)", joining information architecture email lists, attending conferences, attending workshops and talking about web information architecture with other practitioners. There was expression, too, of self-responsibility and initiative for expanding individual knowledge of web information architecture.

Intentional mentoring in the work of web information architecture was evident across many of the organizations in this study. Both external and resident expertise was used in a deliberate way to develop the information architecture capability of others involved in structuring web information. It was a planned and purposeful strategy for acquiring knowledge of web information architecture on the job. Those being mentored were aware that it was in place: 'Yeah and she's mentoring me so I'm getting more skills to understand (Org B)'.

Another practitioner of web information architecture described an ideal situation for progressing his knowledge and expertise. He was undertaking a tertiary course in web information architecture and simultaneously working alongside a specialist information architect in practice. The consultant did not do the work of web information architecture for the organization. Rather, he tutored the individuals in their situated practice and achievement of web information architecture:

> (The consultant) actually did it as a mentoring type thing, specifically the aim of building up seven or eight people across the organization with those skills, so that when he left that wasn't lost. (Org D)

Confidence was instilled in those doing the work of web information architecture by mentoring. Bringing more than just instruction, a specialist mentor brought a buoyant sense of capability.

In this way, the practitioners of web information architecture in large organizations constructed an identity as information professionals with an awareness of best practice and optimal information structures. Yet these perspectives were not shared by all stakeholders with purpose for the enterprise website. The practitioners of web information architecture expressed particular difficulty in implementing the needs and desires of the marketing and professional communication departments.

They noted a tension around what was wanted by marketing and public relations departments, and what they, as information professional, could reasonably achieve. One of the areas of disconnection and discontent was the time-frame of delivering the expectations of the marketing department.

> The tension tends to be, for marketing communication, centred around speed of execution for certain things like—'Make all websites comply with this new template'. Well, this doesn't happen quickly …. I think that there is also tension around the speed of innovation side where the marketing efforts tend to be fairly short-term focus and very, I guess, driven by response cycles—we need this thing now! (Org A)

A fractious relationship between those from a marketing or public relations disciplinary background and those whose focus is on optimising the web information space was revealed. The inability of the web team to fulfil the needs and desires of those with a marketing/public relations focus impacted on the relationship between the two areas and the people within them. One web manager with responsibility for information architecture expressed the difficulty in managing the ongoing extremes of what was wanted by the public affairs department and how it affected his role in managing the web. He was always the one who said *No*, and tensions mounted as a result:

> The relationship with Public Affairs is fraught, Public Affairs still sees the web thing, or particularly sees me as the person who won't let them do anything fun. I'm the one that always says 'No, you've got to do, think about accessibility, you've got to think about the Australian Government Standards, web standards, etc.' (Org B)

The boundary of intent and purpose between communication and information professional were a contested space, for example; "Disagreements around, yes, this creative concept might work in the print medium, but in fact the contrast is not sufficient to be read on a website, that sort of stuff (Org D)". Best practice endeavours, knowledge of theory and method, and an identity as information professional, created a conflicted relationship with practitioners of disciplines with opposing priorities and differing values.

4.5   Practice in SMEs

Those that engaged in the practice of web information architecture in the smaller enterprise were from a professional communication background such as marketing, public relations or journalism, and held qualifications in that field. Strong disciplinary influences on the practice of web information architecture came from the professional communication field. Workplace experiences in political media and public relations, radio journalism, marketing and graphic design were background for the practitioners of web information architecture:

> (m)y career is actually in communication. I'm a journalist by training and I've done a lot of public affairs work in various government agencies and more recently in the community sector (Org J).

A marketing manager in one of the studied SMEs had recently developed and documented an information architecture for implementation by external web developers. She is confident in her ability to design an information architecture for the organization's website yet she has little experience or theoretical knowledge in information organization. She was quick to affirm that her work in the SME is positioned and underpinned by communication and she emphasises a multi-channel and multidisciplinary approach to the external communication for which she has responsibility:

> (m)y role is Marketing Manager. So I look after the communications, primarily external communications, and coordinate advertising, P.R, design work, the website, the whole mix, this whole organization (Org K).

In the process of developing a new site, one of the studied SMEs had recruited an outside agency to take the lead and develop a new web information architecture. "They're pretty highly regarded in Australia as being the leaders of digital strategy, digital advertising and marketing" (Org K). The website of the outside agency emphasised its capability as: "powerful thinking that allows us to connect brands and people like never before". The agency did not claim any expertise in web information architecture. In its outsourcing, the work of web information architecture was placed with communication professionals, rather than specialists from the information discipline.

Unversed in the current theoretical debate around pervasive information architecture, SMEs expressed a cross-channel intention in identifying themselves and informing clients. When information design was commissioned to an external agency, it formed the structural basis for print, web and other channels. Information is of great concern to the practitioners of web information architecture in SMEs, however, disciplinary expertise resides in the printed brochure, which then informs the information structures of the website.

> We're also looking at rebranding with a new logo, and a new image, that's going to go right across the board in prospectuses and everywhere…I think it's really important to work holistically. So the websites not in isolation, you know it's everything … it's the way we present ourselves all the way through. (Org H)

The practice discourse of web information architecture in SMEs includes brochures, copy and branding, indicative of a dominant marketing and communication perspective and theoretical background. Brochures and prospectuses remain an important channel for informing clients. They were, at times, a higher priority than the website:

> The demand for a new prospectus is higher than the website, Xxxx has to produce that prospectus by September, so come September she will actually have a graphic image and organization of data that will probably be the forerunner for the website. It won't have as much deep, rich content, because the website allows you to add so much more. It's the informal method we've used (Org H).

The practitioners of web information architecture in SMEs had not undertaken any formal training or education for their practice. When questioned, they had little knowledge of the theory, methodology or literature. One practitioner of web information architecture reports "no formal or no high degree of sophistication or, you know, knowledge perspective" (Org L). Digital experience in general and long-term engagement with the web as a user, were claimed as sufficient grounding for their practice.

4.6 Discussion

The research reported in this chapter suggests that the activity of web information architecture in large organizations is strongly impacted by professionals and traditions from the information field. Web information architecture methods and theory are known and information architects are employed, either in-house or by commission, to structure web information and to lead, influence and mentor other practitioners.

Yet, an alliance to the information discipline and a desire to conform to the emerging and practical literature for web information architecture, places the practitioner in large organizations in conflict with the marketing communication departments. A disciplinary base with differing needs, approaches, priorities, visions and timeframes is confronted. Whilst one of the seven large organizations studied had found a bounded yet comfortable way of relating with colleagues in marketing communication, in most organizations there was considerable conflict and animosity.

In adhering to an information perspective for web information architecture, practitioners considered other channels for informing as distinct and removed. They were the domain of other departments and responsibility for physical and digital information was polarised. Cross-channel collaborations were not considered or facilitated.

In SMEs, however, a communication professional is most likely to be the practitioner of web information architecture. The expertise of professional information architects is absent in practice. An information disciplinary perspective is replaced by one of communication in the design of information structures for the websites of SMEs. The practitioner of web information architecture in the smaller enterprise brings expertise in digital marketing, experiences in website construction, and a background in communication to the practice. Intuition and common sense replace the skills and theoretical underpinnings of the information professionals.

Yet, cross-channel consideration of information is a normal and comfortable engagement in SMEs. The web is part of a larger communication endeavour. Economies of scale dictate that responsibility for information on the printed brochure and on the website is frequently embodied in a single individual or department. A natural permission is granted for information architecture to embrace, not only the web, but the entire information layer that binds the multiple channels used by an SME to inform its audience. An unexpected opportunity is presented to consider information architecture through a cross-channel lens in the locale of the SME.

Rosenfeld and Morville (2006) built tight bonds between information architecture and the information discipline in their structured methodology for web information architecture in large organizations. The LIS heritage of metadata, taxonomy and search was firmly embedded in their proposal for practice. If the practice of web information architecture was to find a home in an existing discipline, then the information discipline was a strong contender. Its influence on the practice is established.

In recent years, however, information, or an information layer, is heralded as the glue that binds the multiple channels available to the modern and mobile information seeker and new grounds and complexities are presented to the practitioner of information architecture. Current shifts in the practice discourse to cross-channel, pervasive information architecture reignite the emphasis on the multidisciplinary nature of the practice and it continues to elude a comfortable extant disciplinary base. It appears that the practice of information architecture is yet to become a research-informed discipline in its own right.

Those with focused employment in the practice of information architecture continue to struggle to define their practice and to call for a disciplinary base to support their work (for example, Hobbs et al. 2010; Davis 2013). Hobbs et al. (2010) envision a new discipline emerging and see research as the means of its creation. They promote, in particular, practice-based research to transform the practice of information architecture to a discipline with codified and validated knowledge.

Klein (1990, p. 104) describes a discipline thus:

(t)he term discipline signifies the tools, methods, procedures, exempla, concepts, and theories that account coherently for a set of objects or subjects. Over time they are shaped and reshaped by external contingencies and internal intellectual demands. In this manner a discipline comes to organize and concentrate experience into a particular "world view".

Classic or web information architecture has a known subject or domain—the discrete website. With the influence of the information discipline, it was in the process of maturing a set of methods, concepts and theories. In recent years, impacted by external forces of evolving technology, practice leaders of information architecture propose a cross-channel information layer as set of subjects for practice and the quest for appropriate tools, methods and theories begins anew. The disciplinary maturity of information architecture remains elusive.

4.7 Conclusions

The study of situated practice reported in this chapter separates the reality of the activity of information architecture from that prescribed by experts and documented best practice. It focuses on a domain of information architecture that is strongly influenced by prior information traditions—that of information architecture for organizational websites. However, using this approach, the research uncovers surprising vistas of Resmini and Rosati's (2011b) notion of cross-channel information architecture in SMEs and suggests that a firm and institutionalised discipline base for information architecture is still in the making. SMEs have natural tendency to cross-channel information architecture and are revealed as fertile sites for future research. At the same time, large organizations increasing adopt best practice and information traditions in web information architecture, and demonstrate a more focused and siloed approach to information architecture.

References

Bjorkeng, K., Clegg, S., & Pitsis, T. (2009). Becoming (a) practice. *Management Learning, 40*(2), 145–159.

Burford, S. (2011). Complexity and web information architecture. *Journal of the American Society of Information Science and Technology, 62*(10), 2024–2037.

Burford, S. (2014). A grounded theory of the practice of web information architecture in large organizations. *Journal of the American Society of Information Science and Technology* (in press).

Burford, S., & Given, L. (2013). The practitioners of web information architecture in small and medium enterprises. *Journal of Information Architecture* (in press).

Carliner, S. (2008). An interview with Louis Rosenfeld. *Information Design Journal, 16*(2), 101–106.

Charmaz, K. (2006). *Constructing grounded theory*. New York: Sage.

Cook, S., & Brown, J. S. (1999). Bridging epistemologies: The generative dance between organizational knowledge and organizational knowing. *Organization Science, 10*(4), 381–400.

Davis, N. (2013). Information architecture: Beyond web sites, apps, and screens. UX matters. http://www.uxmatters.com/mt/archives/2013/11/information-architecture-beyond-web-sites-apps-and-screens.php. Accessed Dec 2013.

Dey, I. (1999). *Grounding grounded theory*. New York: Academic.

Dillon, A. (2001). Information architectures in search of an identity? *Bulletin of the American Society of Information Science and Technology, 27*(5), 28–29.

Dillon, A., & Turnbull, D. (2005). Information architecture. In M. Drake (Ed.), *Encyclopedia of library and information science*, (pp. 1–9). Boca Raton: Taylor & Francis.

Eisenhardt, K., & Graebner, M. (2007). Theory building from cases: Opportunities and challenges. *Academy of Management Journal, 50*(1), 25–32.

Evernden, R., & Evernden, E. (2003). *Information first: Integrating knowledge and information architecture for business advantage*. London: Butterworth-Heinemann.

Fast, K. (2006). The confluence of research and practice in information architecture. *Bulletin of the American Society of Information Science and Technology, 32*(5), 27.

Geiger, D. (2009). Revisiting the concept of practice: Toward an argumentative understanding of practicing. *Management Learning, 40*(2), 129–144.

Gherardi, S. (2006). *Organizational knowledge: The texture of workplace learning*. London: Blackwell.

Gherardi, S. (2009a). Knowing and learning in practice-based studies: An introduction. *The Learning Organization, 16*(5), 352–359.

Gherardi, S. (2009b). Introduction: The critical power of the 'practice lens'. *Management Learning, 40*(2), 115–128.

Hartley, J. (2004). Case study research. In C. Cassell & G. Symon (Eds.), *Essential guide to qualitative methods in organisational research*, (pp. 323–333). New York: Sage.

Hobbs, J., Fenn, T., & Resmini, A. (2010). Maturing a practice. *Journal of Information Architecture, 2*(1), 37–54.

Klein, J. (1990). *Interdisciplinarity: History, theory, and practice*. Detroit: Wayne State University Press.

Laudon, K., & Laudon, J. (2006). *Management information systems: Managing the digital firm* (9th ed.). Englewood Cliffs: Prentice Hall.

Lawrence, T., & Suddaby, R. (2006). Institutions and institutional work. In S. Clegg, C. Hardy, T. Lawrence, & W. Nord (Eds.), *The sage handbook of organization studies* (2nd ed., pp. 215–254). New York: Sage.

Madsen, D. (2009). Shall we dance? *Journal of Information Architecture, 1*(1), 1–5.

Mahon, B., & Gilchrist, A. (2004). Introduction. In A. Gilchrist & B. Mahon (Eds.), *Information architecture: Designing information environments for purpose*, (pp. xvii–xxii). London: Facet Publishing.

Merriam, S. (1998). *Qualitative research and case study applications in education*. San Francisco: Jossey-Bass.

Morrogh, E. (2002). *Information architecture: An emerging 21st century profession*. Englewood Cliffs: Prentice Hall.

Morville, P. (2004). A brief history of information architecture. In A. Gilchrist & B. Mahon (Eds.), *Information architecture: Designing information environments for purpose*, (pp. xii–xvi). London: Facet Publishing.

Resmini, A., & Rosati, L. (2011a). A Brief History of Information Architecture. *Journal of Information Architecture, 3*(2), 33–45.

Resmini, A., & Rosati, L. (2011b). *Pervasive Information Architecture: Designing Cross-channel User Experiences*. Morgan Kaufmann.

Resmini, A., Byström, K., & Madsen, D. (2009). *Information Architecture Growing Roots-Concerning the. Journal of information architecture*. Bulletin of the American Society of Information Science and Technology, 35(3), 31–33.

Rosenfeld, L. & Morville, P. (1998). Information architecture for the world wide web. Sebastopol, CA: O'Reilly and Associates.

Rosenfeld, L., & Morville, P. (2006). *Information architecture for the world wide web* (3rd ed.). Sebastopol: O'Reilly.

Rouse, J. (2001). Two concepts of practice. In T. Schatzki, K. Knorr-Cetina, & E. von Savigny, (Eds.), *The practice turn in contemporary theory*, (pp. 189–198). London: Routledge.

Shaw, P. (2002). *Changing conversations in organisations: A complexity approach to change*. London: Routledge.

Stair, R., & Reynolds, G. (2008). *Principles of information systems* (8th ed.). Boston: Thomson.

White, M. (2004). Viewpoint: Information architecture. *The Electronic Library, 22*(3), 218–219.

Chapter 5
A Phenomenological Approach to Understanding Information and its Objects

Thomas Wendt

Abstract This paper introduces a phenomenological understanding of information as it relates to technology use. Phenomenology is more commonly applied to the understanding of "things"—or the relationship between things, experience, and cognition—than it is to information studies, but there is much that phenomenological philosophy can contribute to understanding the interactions between humans and information. This paper will focus on how classical and contemporary phenomenological ideas influence our understanding of information, ultimately suggesting a deeper understanding of praxis-based organization and design.

5.1 Phenomenology and Information Architecture

Phenomenology is not traditionally concerned with information. As a practice or philosophical method, it is focused on the question of being, of how individuals *are* in the world. The primary concern is defining what it means *to be*. When we say "the coffee mug is full of coffee," what is the meaning of *is*? While this might seem like a terribly mundane and frustratingly broad object of analysis, it is the rough outline of the phenomenological effort at its inception.

Edmund Husserl, the originator of phenomenology, states that all consciousness is consciousness *of something* (Husserl 2001). This statement, known in phenomenological terminology as "intentionality," grounded all consciousness in its objects. We cannot think of consciousness as divorced from the object of consciousness; the conscious subject and the world of objects are intimately connected.

Phenomenology broke with previous ontological theories based on Cartesian divisions between self and world. For phenomenologists, we understand the world through our engaged dealings with it, as opposed to abstract speculation. That is to say knowledge and understanding can only result from action, or praxis. Theoretical models are decontextualized from real world conditions, while practical methods without theoretical models are pantomime. Praxis is theory-informed practice, and it describes our everyday dealings with the world.

T. Wendt (✉)
Surrounding Signifiers, New York, USA
e-mail: thomas@srsg.co

A. Resmini (ed.), *Reframing Information Architecture,* Human-Computer Interaction Series,   61
DOI 10.1007/978-3-319-06492-5_5, © Springer International Publishing Switzerland 2014

We can think of information in a similar way: information exists for something. Whether it is designed information or information that results from networked consequences of other information, it cannot be examined 'objectively' as a disembodied entity. When we design information spaces, we are designing them for something, for some kind of purpose. When an information architect talks about ontology, they are articulating information's mode of being. Phenomenology is a framework for understanding this mode of being and how humans are embedded and embodied in information spaces.

5.2   Ordering, Enframing, Provoking

Martin Heidegger—a student of Husserl who eventually strayed significantly from his teacher—is arguably the first western philosopher to launch a serious inquiry into the nature of technology. His essay, *The Question Concerning Technology*, had a large impact on subsequent technological analyses. Heidegger's interest was not so much about technological devices but rather to describe what he called the "essence" of technology: what *is* technology? The first step Heidegger takes is to articulate the notion of revealing:

> That revealing that rules in modern technology is a challenging [Herausfordern], which puts to nature the unreasonable demand that it supply energy that can be extracted and stored as such. But does this not hold true for the old windmill as well? No. Its sails do indeed turn in the wind; they are left entirely to the wind's blowing. But the windmill does not unlock energy from the air currents in order to store it (Heidegger 1982).

Simply put, technology is a force that lends access to something we could not otherwise experience. The manner in which a mobile device provides pervasive access to the Internet is the same as the hammer that provides access to driving a nail into wood. This revealing is classified as a challenging, or challenging-forth. It is worth noting that the German word Heidegger uses for 'challenging' is *Herausfordern*, which in certain contexts could also mean 'provocation.' So technology becomes a force that provokes and challenges through revealing.

We should also notice that *Herausfordern* contains the root for the English 'order.' Technology is a challenge to create order within a new way of revealing within a frame:

> Enframing means the gathering together of that setting-upon which sets upon man, i.e., challenges him forth, to reveal the real, in the mode of ordering, as standing-reserve (Heidegger 1982).

Enframing (*Gestell*) functions to gather the world in such a way as to present it in a certain manner, challenging and provoking humans to order it—perhaps to make sense of it. Technology provides the frame through which we see the world as standing-reserve, or a pool of energy we are able to call on at any time to accomplish a goal. This phenomenon is the basis for Heidegger's criticism of modern technology, but it also serves to show that if we want to store technological energy for later purposes, we certainly need to oder it in a way that makes sense later.

5.3   Information Types

It is tempting to say information architecture is part of humanity's answer to technology's call for order—information architects are the brave souls who stand up and say, "we can create order and meaning in the technologically-mediated world!". While partially true, this interpretation does not account for all the nuances within human-technology interaction.

Phenomenology stresses the importance of context. Heidegger's use of the word "dasein" instead of consciousness or subjectivity is exemplary of how he viewed humans' place in the world. Dasein, literally "being-there," is meant to convey the individual's engagement with the world; s/he is not simply *in the world*, but rather is *involved* in the world, existing against a contextual background upon which all behaviors, cognitions, interactions, etc. are contingent. Heidegger opposed Cartesian models of individual consciousness, which posited a strict division between mind and body, self and world. For Heidegger, the individual is completely wrapped up in the world, always in context, never able to be divorced from situations.

Philosopher of technology Albert Borgmann articulated three types of information that serve as the contextual background of everyday life: natural, cultural, and technological (Borgmann 1999). Natural information is information *about* reality. This type of information tells us something about reality; the common example is smoke on the horizon tells us that there is a fire somewhere. Cultural information is information *for* reality. These are conventions like language—closed systems that are designed for a specific purpose, to convey a certain type of meaning. Technological information is information *as* reality. These are instances where technology moves past reality and composes its own hyperreality. Think of how the text message is often perceived as qualitatively better, more useful, and more enjoyable than face-to-face conversation or even a phone call in certain contexts (Fig. 5.1).

Information architects work primarily in the domain of cultural information. While natural information springs forth from the natural world and technological information emerges from complex systems, the cultural domain lends itself to direct manipulation. Cultural information spaces are designed information spaces—that is, they result from systems enacted within them by teleological beings. Dasein's intentionality plays itself out within cultural information; it allows us to interpret and make meaning out of the natural and hyper-natural worlds.

But sense making needs to be facilitated by structures we consciously or unconsciously create in the cultural domain. Borgmann used his model to criticize technology for spiraling out farther and farther from reality (Borgmann 2001). But there is another interpretation of this progression from natural to hyperreal that leaves room for human to take an active role in shaping emergent information.

Taken out of context, Borgmann's model forgets that humans are in the business of actively engaging with their environment. It explains information's mode of being but, on its own, it lacks the means to incorporate real interactions. Don Ihde classified two types of relations with technology as embodied and hermeneutic (Ihde 1990). Embodied relations are those in which the user *acts-through* the object to accomplish something else.

Fig. 5.1 Natural, cultural, technological. (Fire, *left*, designed by A. Adamson, Noun Project. Released under CC BY 3.0. *Center* and *right*, public domain. Noun Project)

This interaction is based on Heidegger's notion of readiness-to-hand (*Zuhanden-heit*), in which a tool becomes an extension of the body—we act through a hammer to drive a nail, through a keyboard to write, through contact lenses to see. Hermeneutic relations are those in which the object is experienced as something other; there is a detachment from bodily relations and the user is conscious of the object as a thing to be analyzed objectively. The hermeneutic relationship is related to Heidegger's idea of the present-at-hand, or a relationship to an object classified by other-ness, or an objective, scientific stance. In embodiment relations, the focus is on an end goal, whereas in hermeneutic relations the focus is on the object itself.

The common example is that of a hammer. When one is using a hammer, one is acting through the hammer to drive a nail. The hammer itself is not a focal point in the interaction until the hammer breaks. At this point, the user needs to cope with the broken-ness of the hammer by finding a new one or figuring out a way to continue use in a modified way. When the hammer functions properly, it is in an embodied relation with the user; when it breaks, it becomes the object of attention and shifts to a hermeneutic relation.

5.4   Modern Interaction Styles

Modern technology is a bit more complicated. Take the example of making coffee. If one is using an electric machine that runs on a timer, one might prepare coffee the night before and set the timer for the same time as one's alarm clock. In this scenario, the coffee maker begins brewing coffee as the user is waking up, creating a choreography (Klyn 2010) between the user and the end goal of attaining coffee. Is the user in an embodied relationship with the coffee machine, since the interaction is automated and removed from conscious awareness? Or is it hermeneutic, since its object-ness is necessary to enable automation? How does using an electric coffee maker compare to a pour-over dripper? The dripper might allow for more of an embodied relation, as it incorporates the user's hand to into the manual interaction of pouring water over grounds, but it also enables a ritual that results in experiencing coffee as an object of analysis.

Embodied   Hermeneutic

Fig. 5.2 Embodied, hermeneutic. (*Left*, Public Domain, Noun Project. *Right*, Google Glass, Damion. Noun Project)

Another way to think about embodied and hermeneutic relations is that embodied technologies rely primarily on natural information and hermeneutic technologies rely on a mixture of natural, cultural, and technological information. A common embodied technology is a pair of eyeglasses. The user wears eyeglasses to see the world as it *really is*, often forgetting about the glasses completely—assuming they fit properly, are not smudged, etc.—as they go about their everyday dealings. The glasses become an extension of the body, used in order to see natural information in the world.

A modern twist on eyeglasses, something like Google Glass, takes a very different approach. While structurally similar, Glass allows the user to *see* much more than what is *really there*. Glass holds the promise of being one of the first "invisible" interfaces, able to be seamlessly incorporated into everyday life, but at the time of writing, it is still in its infancy. Glass is an object of awe, a designed spectacle that, in its current state, could never become incorporated into the body as prescription lenses have. While eyeglasses function on natural information, Glass relies on the designed hyperreality of designed information spaces (Fig. 5.2).

It is all too easy to make a moral judgment within this distinction: embodied relations are preferable to hermeneutic relations because they are more 'natural.' This conclusion assumes that these categories stand in opposition. Instead, we can think of them as ends of a spectrum. No object is ever static in its relation to the user. Eyeglasses will break, smudge, hinges will stretch, screws fall out... all leading to a movement from the embodied side to the hermeneutic (Fig. 5.3).

The relationship to information moves from natural to designed. As the glasses become an object of analysis, they are no longer looked *through* but rather are looked *at*. In a similar interaction with Glass, eventually (if all goes well for Google) the device will draw less attention from others and will have better applications that allow for embodied use.

Context-aware computing has always had embodied relations as its end goal. If a computing system can have specialized knowledge of a user's contextual situation, it can organize information in a way that significantly decreases the amount of conscious, intentional interaction the user has with the system. While this dream has not yet been realized, a number of products are currently on the market that aim to account for user context.

One example is Aviate, an Android launch screen that organizes information based on several criteria: location, time, movement, application category. The "morning routine" category surfaces the applications that a user commonly views

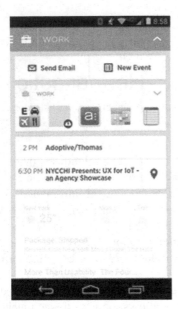

Fig. 5.3 Aviate screens on Android

in the morning along with weather information and the first meeting of the day. Likewise, "work" senses that the user is currently in an office or other place of work and serves apps associated with that setting.

Location-based categories use ambient location information to take a best guess on the user's physical location and serve applications related to where s/he is—i.e., Yelp if at a restaurant, Delta app if at an airport, etc. While at first this functionality elicits strong hermeneutic feelings of a technological "other," once the system becomes smarter and more utility-focused, it quickly moves toward the embodied side of the spectrum and dominates the interaction style. This movement is a direct result of a working adaptive information architecture. Even if the information is organized in the same way, the user's experience of the information changes over time as it moves through the embodied-hermeneutic spectrum.

Aviate runs on all three types of information. Natural information feeds into the strictly utilitarian features: weather forecast and the first meeting of the day serves as information about reality, or at least the day's reality. Cultural information is the foundation for allows the user to make sense of the various iterations of the launch screen: changing from "morning routine" to "going somewhere" (in motion) to "home" makes sense because of the cultural information that feeds the transition. Technological information frames the entire experience: a piece of technology that uses context to adapt information spaces takes on hyperreal qualities. All these types of information expose themselves in different modes at different times.

5.5   Affordances

We have so far traced a path from Heidegger's distinction between present-at-hand and ready-to-hand, to Borgmann's information types, and finally to Ihde's interaction styles. The common thread so far has been the line drawn between self and other. A core question each of these philosophers have attempted to answer is: To what extent are objects and information incorporated into the body verses remaining a part of the external world? It seems that the answer to this question is the holy grail of information architecture.

James J. Gibson, a psychologist who studied visual perception, might disagree slightly with the supposed urgency of the question. He was the first to articulate the theory of affordances, or the aspects of an environment that allow for objects within that environment to be used (Gibson 1986). A door affords passage to a new space, water affords bathing, a ball affords throwing, etc. Affordances are invitations, perhaps even provocations or challenges to take action. They are indications of the conditions of possibility that exist for an object; they do not dictate action but rather suggest it.

For Gibson, affordances are the missing link between self and world, body and environment, human and tool:

> When in use, a tool is a sort of extension of the hand, almost an attachment to it or part of the user's own body, and thus no longer a part of the environment of the user. But when not in use the tool is simply a detached object of the environment, graspable and portable, to be sure, but nevertheless external to the observer. This capacity to attach something to the body suggests that the boundary between the animal and the environment is not fixed at the surface of the skin but can shift. More generally it suggests that the absolute duality of 'objective' and 'subjective' is false. When we consider the affordances of things, we escape this philosophical dichotomy (Gibson 1986).

While an affordance exists as part of the external environment, it allows for ready-to-hand interaction that results in the user incorporating it into his/her own body. We should recall Maurice Merleau-Ponty's examination of the blind man's stick; through the walking stick, the blind man is able to sense his environment and avoid obstacles. His entire "visual" world exists at the end of that stick.

Similarly, when we use a knife to cut a loaf of bread, the knife fades into the contextual background as we focus on cutting slices to the desired thickness, and thus the knife becomes incorporated into the user's hand. The blade's affordance for cutting and the handle for gripping bridges the gap between body and world, subject and object. The distinction starts to dissolve when we consider affordances as a middle ground:

> An affordance cuts across the dichotomy of subjective-objective and helps us to understand its inadequacy. It is equally a fact of the environment and a fact of behavior. It is both physical and psychical, yet neither. An affordance points both ways, to the environment and to the observer (Gibson 1986).

Recall Heidegger's notion of technology as a revealing or challenging forth: affordances are the means by which technology reveals itself as not entirely *other*. The middle ground an affordance grants new possibilities for classification and ordering objects according to praxis instead of ontological or taxonomic categories:

> The fact that a stone is a missile does not imply that it cannot be other things as well. It can be a paperweight, a bookend, a hammer, or a pendulum bob [...] If you know what can be done with a graspable detached object, what it can be used for, you can call it whatever you please. The theory of affordances rescues us from the philosophical muddle of assuming fixed classes of objects, each defined by its common features and then given a name (Gibson 1986).

Gibson does not elaborate too much on this point, but it is significant. Humans are very used to classifying objects based on the assumption that they are external to our sense of self. What is often missed in this approach is their potential for action and incorporation as embodied, ready-to-hand objects. A new way to think about organization is to classify objects not as they what *are* but as what they *do*.

5.6   Alternate Classification Systems

In physical spaces, there are implications for objects we have already discussed. Ontologically, eyeglasses and Google Glass are similar. They are eyewear. They are worn on the face, and one looks through them to enhance sight—either by correcting a defect and allowing a user to see the world as it is, or by adding to the world and allowing the user to see what the world is lacking. This last point gets to affordance-based classification.

In terms of what they do, eyeglasses and Glass are completely different. While eyeglasses correct a defect in the user, Glass fills a void in the world. Their ontological nature is similar, while their praxis is quite different.

Many digital products are using this classification system already. Some information-heavy websites, for example, have adopted a task-based navigation to filter content based on what a user needs to accomplish. Aviate does something similar when it organizes information and applications based on the user's context. Time, location, and movement play a large role in what information is presented and when. The system guesses what the users needs to do based on where s/he is, time of day, whether s/he is in motion, upcoming calendar events, etc., and affords actions based on this information.

A phenomenological, praxis-based approach to information architecture would account for the user's context, actions needed at different times, and adaptation to various scenarios. Hopefully, the phenomenological tip of the iceberg this paper presents will spark more conversation on how to design praxis-based systems. Connecting Gibson's theory of affordances with its phenomenological background can offer IA new ways to think about things like taxonomy and ontology. To suggest that we understand things not by what they *are* but rather by what they *do* is a major ontological shift. I believe these same insights can be applied to our relationship with information.

References

Borgmann, A. (1999). *Holding on to reality*. Chicago: University of Chicago Press.
Borgmann, A. (2001). Opaque and articulate design. *International Journal of Technology and Design Education, 11*(1), 5–11.
Gibson, J. J. (1986). *The ecological approach to visual perception*. Evanston: Routledge.
Heidegger, M. (1982). *The question concerning technology, and other essays*. New York: Harper Perennial.
Husserl, E. (2001). *Logical investigations* (Vol. 1). Evanston: Routledge.
Ihde, D. (1990). *Technology and the lifeworld: From garden to earth* (No. 560). Bloomington: Indiana University Press.
Klyn, D. (2010). Explaining information architecture. http://vimeo.com/8866160. Accessed Jan 2014.

Chapter 6
Toward a Culturally Focused Information Architecture

David Fiorito

Abstract In the course of a few decades, beginning in the mid-1970s when the first consumer-focused computers started to appear in homes, software has moved from being a curiosity embraced by a minority of early adopters to being a natural extension of human activity and a part of daily life in nearly every corner of the globe. In the mid-2000s, networked computing moved from the desktop and laptop computer and into the pockets of people the world over. While culture hit a flection point and technology was going through this burst of rapid evolution from desktop to mobile computing, the discipline of information architecture went through its own developmental challenges. The period from 2007 to 2009 saw the field change and face a sobering challenge to its very relevance, and the infusion of a new spirit and direction. This rebirth of information architecture has been marked by a renewed focus on the fundamentals of the discipline as seen in the work and research of Andrea Resmini and Luca Rosati and their exploration of its application across the many channels through which we encounter information, in Andrew Hinton's studies of the contexts in which people use the systems we design, and in the work of Dan Klyn. This chapter adds one more facet to this new spirit of information architecture—culture. Culture is a critical component: we design the tools that people will use within their own complex cultural contexts. New methods and approaches to our practice are needed, as those that we currently use lack a focus on culture and its dynamics: this paper argues that the academic practice of anthropology can lend information architecture those tools.

6.1 From Wired Individuals to Networked Cultures

In order to understand how anthropology can help us move information architecture forward, we must first examine the transformational processes that both technology and the discipline experienced at the turn of the twenty-first century. The physiology of the developing brain offers a good metaphor.

D. Fiorito (✉)
EPAM, Empathy Lab, Philadelphia, PA, USA
e-mail: crosswiredmind@me.com

A. Resmini (ed.), *Reframing Information Architecture,* Human-Computer Interaction Series, 71
DOI 10.1007/978-3-319-06492-5_6, © Springer International Publishing Switzerland 2014

While still in the womb, and before our eyes have fully formed, bursts of neuro-logical activity fire from the retina and cascade through the sections of the brain that will later become responsible for visual processing. The neurobiologists at Yale that first observed this phenomena believe that the brain is wiring itself for sight (Ackman et al. 2012). Throughout the development of the brain in utero such processes occur repeatedly, while neurons form, self-organize, and begin to fire. Complex structures develop and complex neural activity accelerates.

In a similar way, we have seen bursts of binary code cascade through emerging digital networks from the SAGE air defense system of the 1950s, to ARPANET in 1969, to the advent of the World Wide Web: we passed through a formative period during which we were being wired for a networked world. And while it may seem now as if we have been networked for many years, it was only recently that we could say that we have passed through the developmental stages of our digital life and can now "see" for the first time.

6.2   The Tipping Point

Our digital lives were once separated from the rest of our lives by the length of the power cord that connected our bulky computers to an electrical outlet. The computer sat on a table or desk in a bedroom, basement, or office. To access our digital lives we had to go to where the computer was with the exception of some governmental and educational institutions, there were no real networks for the average person.

When digital connectivity finally arrived, it was carried over phone lines via a very slow modem between an individual computer and one that acted as a hub of activity. The nascent communities that grew out of services like CompuServe and other BBS destinations bore little resemblance to the networks of social relationships we maintained in our day-to-day lives.

These were the early bursts of activity that were wiring us for the transformation from wired individuals to networked cultures, and while it could be argued no single tipping point can be unequivocally identified, the Apple iPhone becoming generally available in June 2007 certainly set off a wave of mobile device adoption that was unprecedented. According to the Pew Internet & American Life Project, 75 % of adults owned a mobile phone (Pew Research Center 2013). By July 2007, there were 9 million smartphone owners in the US according to ComScore, 4 % of adults who owned mobile phones at the time (ComScore 2012). As of 2013, 91 % of adults own a mobile phone, and 56 % of adults own a smart phone (Pew Research Center 2013).

While there had already been smart phones on the market prior to Apple's iPhone, Apple's market share expanded so rapidly that by 2011, just 4 years after it was launched, the iPhone had 30 % of the market (ComScore 2012). More importantly, the iPhone and its operating system iOS were designed for the average consumer rather than for the business professional. It was computing on the go for the masses: the iPhone was accessible and quickly became even fashionable.

But technology alone does not make the arrival of the iPhone a watershed event. Its cultural impact comes through its use as a hub of communication. The ability to use a single device for phone, SMS, and email is powerful, but there were devices that could do that before the iPhone arrived. It was the ability to install applications on the iPhone that made a big difference. The applications that would have the biggest cultural impact were those that allowed us not only to conduct person-to-person communication, but also to build and manage large social networks. The iPhone, and later the Android phone, were devices that could be used to extend our very identities out into a broader world.

The two largest social networking applications launched less than 2 years after the arrival of the iPhone. After Facebook launched an iPhone App its user base doubled, reaching 100 million by August of 2008 and beginning a period of unprecedented growth that crossed the 1 billion user mark within 5 years.

Our digital culture was organizing itself, connections were being made and what had been bursts of activity transformed into a constant flow of information. Our cultural lives had been primed, and the tipping point or points had been passed. Software in all of its forms was now beginning to be used to "mediate, supplement, augment, monitor, regulate, facilitate, and ultimately produce collective life" and "shape people's daily interactions and transactions, and mediate all manner of practices in entertainment, communication, and mobilities" (Kitchen and Dodge 2011, p. 9).

The growth and proliferation of mobile devices in subsequent years led to a 10 % drop in the reported ownership of desktop computers (Pew Research Center 2013), the growth of social media, and, even more striking, the appearance of online communities focused on specific sub-cultures. From the knitters of Ravelry, to the AR-15 enthusiasts of ARFCOM, to the subversives of 4chan, everyone was finding their cultural niche and home online.

6.3   Culture Matters

What is critical to understand about this mobile device driven transformation is that its importance does not reside in the creation of some new cybernetic culture (though certain sub-cultures clearly spawned from it). Like other changes in material culture before it, and especially media-related ones such as the commercial telephone service, broadcast radio and television, the digital leap of 2007 did not merely introduce a new layer to our culture: software became a natural, albeit complex, extension of it. Like the invention of written language as an extension of spoken language, software and the hardware it runs on had now become a normalized, organic part of our being human:

> (A)ll that which can be ultimately reduced to binary code (…) the digital, as all material culture, is more than a substrate; it is becoming a constitutive part of what makes us human (Miller and Horst 2012, pp. 3–4).

Indeed we cannot separate our culture from the systems we use to extend it. In the closing of "The Hidden Dimension", Edward T. Hall writes:

No matter how hard man tries it is impossible for him to divest himself of his own culture, for it has penetrated to the roots of his nervous system and determines how he perceives the world. Most of culture lies hidden and is outside voluntary control, making up the warp and weft of human existence. Even when the small fragments of culture are elevated to awareness, they are difficult to change, not only because they are so personally experienced but because people cannot act or interact at all in any meaningful way except through the medium of culture (Hall 1966, p. 188).

6.4   Culture Defined

Let us take a step back to look at the broader picture in order to understand what culture is to help us understand the deeper implications of this software enabled transformation.

Anthropologist James P. Spradley wrote one of the most concise and powerful definitions of culture as "the acquired knowledge people use to interpret experience and generate behavior" (Spradley 1980, p. 6). While brief, his statement is packed with implications and consequences. Spradley described culture as having three broad components: the things people do (cultural behavior), the things people know (cultural knowledge), and the things people make and use (cultural artifacts). Of these three it is our cultural knowledge that drives the cycle of interpretation and behavior. Clifford Geertz describes cultural knowledge, "not as complexes of concrete behavior patterns (…) but as a set of control mechanisms—plans, recipes, rules, instructions (what computer engineers call 'programs')—for the governing of behavior" (Geertz 1973, p. 44).

Cultural knowledge is acquired through the process of enculturation—lessons taught to us by others both explicitly and implicitly (Kottak 2012, p. 18). While the vast majority of enculturation occurs early on in life, it does continue throughout adulthood as individuals become exposed to, and become a part of, different subcultures. Spradley illustrates this process in his discussion on finding ideal informants for his research into the culture of cocktail waitresses (Spradley 1979, p. 47). He describes his conversations with a relatively new waitress who was just learning her job: she did not have the same depth of knowledge regarding that particular cultural context as the more experienced waitresses, but by the time his fieldwork was complete she had become a much more knowledgeable insider—a fully enculturated member of that particular sub-culture with enough cultural knowledge to be able to explain their culture to him.

Some cultural knowledge can be easily communicated by members of a particular culture: this is called explicit cultural knowledge. It includes a wide array of topics and subjects, including among others kinship structures (Spradley 1980, p. 7), and traditions, norms, and expected behaviors (Kottak 2012, p. 18).

But there is also a body of cultural knowledge that cannot be consciously communicated. This is called tacit cultural knowledge, and can only be understood through observation and inference (Spradley 1980, p. 11). A prime example of tacit cultural knowledge at work is seen in Edward T. Hall's seminal work on proxemics—his study of the interpersonal distances used in social interactions (Hall 1966).

6.5   The Importance of Cultural Knowledge

To become more focused on designing for the cultural contexts of the users, information architects must be able to understand it the same way anthropologists do. Granted, it is common for anthropologists to conduct at least one full year immersed in ethnographic research, while information architects will have substantially less time than that, but that does not mean that ethnographic methods will not be valuable.

Even with limited time, good research can still gather insights and formulate findings that go beyond the behavior of individual users and expand out to the understanding of our users' culture. The fundamental principles and activities found in Spradley's ethnographic interview (Spradley 1979) and participant observation techniques (Spradley 1980), or in W. Penn Handwerker's methods for quick ethnography (Handwerker 2001), are readily adaptable to the short bursts of research typical in the professional lives of information architects.

The goal of these methods, and the tremendous value they add to information architecture, is to reach an understanding of cultural knowledge, both tacit and explicit, through observation and inference.

6.5.1   Explicit Cultural Knowledge

Because explicit cultural knowledge is something people can articulate, the observation of language use is the most direct method of gaining an understanding of it. Language is the richest system for conveying cultural meaning, as it is used to describe all other systems of encoded cultural meaning (Spradley 1979, p. 99). Spradley's own most notable ethnographic work, "You Owe Yourself a Drunk: An Ethnography of Urban Nomads" (Spradley 1970), is a masterful example of examining language use, specifically the folk taxonomy of skid row tramps, in order to decode systems of meaning found in explicit cultural knowledge.

When he started his fieldwork, Spradley noticed that tramps used three distinct modes of speech—dialects used in specific contexts. When speaking amongst themselves they used terms and syntax that were very different from the language they used with social workers. Dealing with the court system brought in yet another distinct mode of speech. When the implications of this dialectical pluralism became clear to him, Spradley decided to decode them.

It was not an easy process: his attempts to understand the rich language of tramps were plagued by a phenomenon he called translation competence—the tramps were translating their own unique dialect into terms that they believed he would understand. Rather than helping Spradley to understand their culture, this was constantly causing misunderstandings to crop up.

Spradley exemplifies this with the example of a basic question they have to answer often and of its implications. When a social worker asks tramps where they live, tramps will translate that to mean a "permanent home", and so they will answer that they do not have a home. Thus they are labeled as being "homeless", with all manner of derogatory connotation and shame attached to the term. Spradley observed that tramps never identified themselves as "homeless" when they spoke with other tramps. Their native taxonomy reflected a completely different worldview that the social workers and other professionals were missing.

In order to compensate for and eliminate translation competence as an issue and get to the heart of tramp culture through language use, Spradley developed a detailed, multi-step interview technique subsequently published in "The Ethnographic Interview" (Spradley 1979). Through this process he was able to get the tramps to use their native terminology, record it, break it down, and build a complex record of the relationships and meaning of terms in the tramps' native taxonomy. In doing so, Spradley was able to understand their culture, and its focus on challenges such as finding a safe place to sleep. He discovered that far from being "homeless", the men of skid row had a deep and complex understanding of not only where to sleep ("making a flop"), but of the relative merits and drawbacks of various types of flops.

6.5.2   Tacit Cultural Knowledge

Some cultural knowledge though cannot be communicated or decoded, as it is only tacitly understood by members of a culture. In fact, the existence of this form of cultural knowledge is often denied as existing at all. This tacit cultural knowledge can only be observed. For example, the distance between people in a given social context varies from culture to culture but the rules that determine it only become noticeable when members of different cultures find themselves in close proximity.

In his ground breaking work on proxemics, Hall identified four meaningful distances: intimate, personal, social, and public (Hall 1966, pp. 116–125). These are strictly codified within a certain culture. For example, personal distance is from 18 to 30 in. at its closest—the distance at which there is no visual distortion—and 30 and 48 in. at its furthest, or just beyond reach. At this distance, physical contact is unlikely, but one can still make out the fine details of physical characteristics like the size of someone's pupils or fine wrinkles in the skin.

Variations between different social groups are sizeable, but they are not explicitly articulated. Hall observed that in Arab culture, the rules for personal distance are often set by the sense of smell. Where Americans tend to hold conversation at a distance far enough not to smell another's breath, casual conversation in the Arab world tends to be close enough for interlocutors to smell and feel each other's breath (Hall 1966, p. 159).

These are rules that people Hall observed and spoke to could not directly communicate, to the point of claiming that no such rules existed. To understand tacit knowledge, one must be able to observe the context in order to be able to decode and interpret implicit behavior.

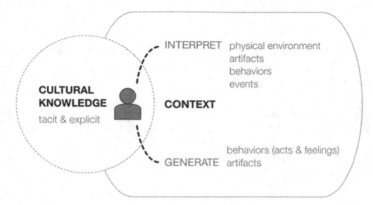

Fig. 6.1 Interpreting experience and generating behavior. Adapted from Spradley 1980, p. 8

6.6   Interpretation & Generation

Because we cannot directly tap into the body of cultural knowledge, we must settle for observing the operation of cultural knowledge. In any given cultural context, individuals will experience (and interact with) the physical environment, cultural artifacts, behaviors, and events. All of these will be interpreted by their cultural knowledge. But individuals are not just passive actors: they also generate behaviors, acts, feelings, and even artifacts in response to their own interpretations (Fig. 6.1).

The key to understanding this cycle is through meaning (Spradley 1980, pp. 8–9). Spradley explains that sociologists George Herbert Mead and Charles Horton Cooley developed a theory that "explain(s) human behavior in terms of meanings". Herbert Blumer, a student of Mead, called this theory symbolic interactionism and articulated three key premises of symbolic interactionism:

1. Our interactions with things are based on the meaning that those things hold for us.
2. The meaning of things is formed through social interactions with others.
3. We use an interpretive process to handle and modify meaning when we encounter a thing.

Spradley holds that explicit and tacit cultural knowledge is formed through social interactions, and that it is used to both generate behavior and emotions, as well as to shape material culture. It also allows us, as Blumer points out, to interpret our experience of the behavior of others, our physical environment, as well as the things we encounter in material culture.

Here we can draw a parallel. The anthropologist observes cultural behavior, the artifacts of material culture, and listens to speech events to build a set of inferences regarding their meaning in order to understand culture and ultimately write an ethnographic description of cultural knowledge in action. The task of the information architect is very similar, with the exception of the final step which is to design artifacts and events that will enter into the interpretation of experience (Fig. 6.2).

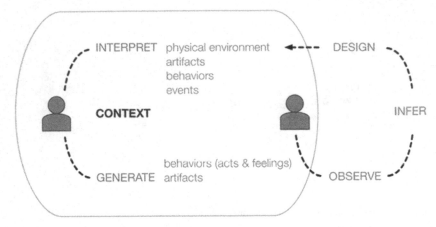

Fig. 6.2 Observe, infer, design

6.7 Language as the Key to Meaning

Clifford Geertz, one of this century's most influential American anthropologists, and a strong supporter of symbolic anthropology, wrote that he believed, with Max Weber, that

> man is an animal suspended in webs of significance he himself has spun (…) I take culture to be those webs, and the analysis of it to be therefore not an experimental science in search of law but an interpretive one in search of meaning (Geertz 1973, p. 5).

To Geertz, the anthropologist is primarily concerned with understanding those "webs of significance" and decoding their meaning. That is the only way to truly gain an insider's view of a culture. Because we cannot directly access cultural knowledge other than our own, we can only rely on observations and our ability to infer the meaning of them. Spradley considers meaning as being "directly expressed in language" and often "taken for granted" by those who speak it. As such, in some cases meaning only comes "indirectly through word and action" (Spradley 1979, p. 5). Or, as linguistic anthropologist Laura M. Ahearn puts it, "every aspect of language is socially influenced and culturally meaningful" (Ahearn 2012, p. 52).

In the view of linguistic anthropology, decoding culture and understanding those "webs of significance" that Geertz equates with culture is accomplished through the study of language with a focus on use. In her introductory text, Ahearn breaks down the study of language into five key components: phonology, the study of the component sounds in a language (or gestures in the case of sign languages); morphology, the study of the structure of individual words; syntax, the study of sentence structure and grammar; semantics, the study of the meaning of words and sentences; pragmatics, the study of the contextual use of language.

The first three of these are the primary concern of linguists: their interest lies completely with structural elements that can be objectively examined and evaluated. They emphasize the "what" over the "why", whereas the understanding of culture requires us to emphasize the "why" over the "what".

Decoding cultural symbols and identifying the coding rules uncovers the patterns in a culture's web of significance. This is critical because

> practices of language use shapes patterns of communication, formulate categories of social identity and group membership, organize large-scale cultural beliefs and ideologies, and, in conjunction with other semiotic practices, equip people with common cultural representations of their natural and social worlds (Society for Linguistic Anthropology 2014).

6.8   Anthropologists & Information Architects

It is here that the world of the anthropologist and the information architect show an interconnection and parallel concerns. If anthropologists can uncover cultural meaning by decoding patterns of language use that "organize large-scale cultural beliefs and ideologies" and "equip people with common cultural representations of their natural and social worlds", then certainly information architects would be well served to learn to do the same, as the systems of organization, navigation, and categorization that are at the core of the practice (Rosenfeld and Morville 1998) are indeed language being used in context.

The use of software is an act of language use. Better yet, the use of software is completely inseparable from the use of language. I am not referring to the code behind the interface here: from the earliest command line interfaces to the hyperlinks of the World Wide Web, software has relied on language and meaningful visual clues to allow a human being to operate and make sense of it.

The networked culture of post 2007 is also a culture that seamlessly conjugates being connected and being online with being mobile through the many different locations we encounter through the day. Andrea Resmini and Luca Rosati posit that through this blend of the digital and the physical, what they call cross-channel ecosystems, we are now living "in a world where relationships with people, places, objects, and companies are shaped by semantics and not (mostly, or only) by physical proximity" (Resmini and Rosati 2011, p. 35).

This is why the notion of decoding "common cultural representations" in the "webs of significance" formed by language use is especially critical to the work of information architects. The software, systems, and services that we design must align with our users' cultural knowledge, both explicit and tacit. The semantics that shape their relationships must be reflected in our designs and expressed in their native language or they will not easily use, or readily adopt, what we have created because they will not recognize it as their own.

Here is where the discipline of information architecture shows a gap—a cultural gap. Or rather a gap in our tools, methods, approaches, and skills that do not account for, or enable us to decode and understand, "the acquired knowledge people use to interpret experience and generate behavior" that is culture.

I posit that given the ongoing post-2007 transformation from a collection of wired individuals to networked cultures, it behooves us to acknowledge that gap, recognize the value of filling it, and then proceed to fill it.

6.9   The Continuing Evolution of Information Architecture

In the 1990s, information architecture largely reflected the technology of the time. In the early days of the World Wide Web, we were in desperate need of organization as webpages, and the hypertext links that connected them, multiplied rapidly with little regard for frameworks and order. Novelty and innovation kept our wired world moving forward even when what we were creating online did not feel particularly aligned with our cultural knowledge.

All the same, the notion that software in all of its forms (applications, webpages, operating systems) needed to be more than well-structured and useable was beginning to become patently obvious as competition heated up for the attention of a growing crowd of wired individuals, and commercial dominance in the proliferating nodes of the Internet. As more and more people from every corner of the world were being connected, the need for our digital world to reflect the needs, languages, esthetics, and expectations of an enormously diverse group of users became apparent. Even so, understanding culture was still not considered an imperative. Instead our focus shifted and expanded as the notion of user experience design grew.

6.10   The Rise of User Experience

October of 2002 saw the publication of Jesse James Garrett's "The Elements of User Experience". Based on an earlier one page diagram, the book placed information architecture within a larger framework that included business strategy, product management, interaction design, information design, and visual design. All of these disciplines would work together to take software from "abstract" to "concrete" through phases that would lay down the strategy, scope, structure, skeleton, and surface layers. The focus of all of this activity was the end user of the software being created.

Garrett would close the loop in his rather famous 2009 plenary (Garrett 2009). In his view, the traditional role of the information architect was far too limited and too tied to the specific medium of the Web. The same, he believed, was true of interaction designers. He saw the need to focus our design work beyond the screen and into the realm described in Kitchin & Dodge's Code/Space, in a way that was no longer focused on a specific medium, but rather in a "a medium-independent or cross-media way". Garrett saw the implication of the developments that unfolded over the previous 2 years—the emergence of networked cultures. But he, like many in the field, still overlooked, misunderstood, or underestimated the impact of culture on design.

The simple broadening from information architecture to user experience design was also a well-meaning but ultimately inadequate response to the emergence of networked cultures. While Garrett exhorted the field to focus on the wider but more ephemeral notion of experience, what changed culture is the unprecedented presence of computation using binary code, something digital anthropology recognizes. As for the experience of using a tool, we have been doing that since we fashioned our first crude prosthesis from wood, bone, hide, and stone.

User experience, to the extent that it can be designed, is the work of teams of specialized individuals, none of whom should be considered to be the "user experience designer". Software is the primary medium we use today to shape new tools. Let the industrial designers and engineers focus on the hardware that is part of the user experience. Let designers and marketers craft the overarching notion of brand identity and experience. And let all of those composers, authors, film makers, and countless other creative professionals design their own contributions to the user experience. But if there is software used within a broader experienced context, or as the focus of a specific context of use, then that is the domain of the information architects, interaction designers, visual designers, and content strategists who shape the digital aspects of those experiences.

6.11   Recasting Information Architecture

In his 2013 presentation at the IA Summit, Dan Klyn showcased the result of his work practicing and teaching information architecture. The way he frames information architecture is not as much a break from the work of Wurman or Rosenfeld and Morville, as it is a clear evolution of that prior work and perhaps a reaction to the challenge posed by Garrett's 2009 declaration that "(t)here are no information architects. There are no interaction designers. There are only, and only ever have been, user experience designers".

Klyn structures his view of information architecture around three core concepts: ontology, taxonomy, and choreography (Klyn 2010). Ontology refers to the "rules and patterns that govern the meaning of what we intend to communicate". It is the job of the information architect to discover, define, and articulate those rules and patterns. Taxonomy focuses on "developing systems and structures for what everything's called, where everything's sorted and for the relationships between labels and categories". Choreography is the structure created to foster "specific types of movement and interaction—anticipating the way users and information want to flow and making affordances for change over time".

Like Garrett's user experience design, Hinton's linkosophy (Hinton 2008), and Resmini and Rosati's ubiquitous ecologies and pervasive information architectures (Resmini and Rosati 2009), Klyn's view of information architecture takes on a tone of medium neutrality. Ontology, taxonomy, and choreography apply to any system in which information is communicated and used. All the same, while Klyn clearly hints at the necessity for a deeper understand of human culture, no explicit connection is voiced. This is the step I outline here.

6.12   The Cultural Implications of Ontology, Taxonomy, and Choreography

Because of the relative vicinity of their core concerns, aligning the methods and approaches of anthropology and Klyn's view of information architecture to explicitly address cultural implications results in a relatively simple process of adaptation.

The process of discovering, defining, and articulating the rules and patterns that govern the rules for communicating meaning in Klyn's notion of ontology mimics the process Spradley describes in his ethnographic interview methodology. One of the key concepts in Spradley's method is the relational theory of meaning. Spradley asserts that "cultural meaning systems are encoded in symbols" (Spradley 1979, p. 99), symbols being anything that refers to something else.

Language is the primary symbolic system: "(l)anguage can be used to talk about all other encoded symbols". The only way to decode these symbols is by uncovering the pattern of relationships between them. In other words, Klyn's key to ontology, those "rules and patterns that govern the meaning of what we intend to communicate", is the information architecture equivalent of Spradley's ethnographic interview techniques.

Rather than "developing systems and structures for what everything's called, where everything's sorted and for the relationships between labels and categories", Klyn's take on taxonomy, I argue that the systems and structures of taxonomy are inherent in, and discovered through, the decoding of the "rules and patterns" of ontology. As Spradley puts it, "cultural meaning systems are encoded in symbols", and that, "the meaning of any symbol is its relationship to other symbols" (Spradley 1979, p. 99).

Finally, it is in the notion of choreography that information architecture finds its greatest expression. The inferred understanding of the users' culture helps generate a software-based artifact that they themselves would have produced and that in turn can produce change within that culture. The biggest challenge for information architecture will not be decoding the cultural aspects of ontology or taxonomy as those frame explicit cultural knowledge, rooted in language use and that can be directly observed through interviews and participant observation. The more difficult task will be to understand the users' tacit cultural knowledge—the behaviors and expectations that they themselves are unaware of.

Certainly the practice of participant observation, essentially a variant of contextual inquiry, or similar methods are well suited to produce the right environment for cultural inferences to be gleaned regarding the pragmatics of software use. In that sense, choreography is as much about meaning as ontology and taxonomy.

6.13   Conclusions

It is important at this point to revisit Geertz and his idea that "man is an animal suspended in webs of significance he himself has spun" (Geertz 1973, p. 5).

In the case of software use within networked cultures, the information architect, very much like Geertz's anthropologist, uses an interpretive science in an effort to understand the users. We cannot assume that our users share our culture knowledge, or that we can shape software for ourselves that they will readily adopt. We may speak the same language, but like the misunderstood tramps labeled as "homeless" our users undoubtedly have a native ontology, taxonomy, and choreography that they simply translate for us when we strike out to conduct our user research.

By adopting anthropological methods and approaches, information architecture can fill this gap in its practice, moving from being user-centered to being culturally focused. To become fluent in the ontology, taxonomy, and choreography of users, information architects need to focus on decoding the systems of cultural meaning in their patterns of language use and become conversant with the cultural knowledge that drives them.

References

Ackman, J. B., Burbridge, T. J., & Crair, M. C. (2012). Retinal waves coordinate patterned activity throughout the developing visual system. *Nature, 490*(7419), 219–225.

Ahearn, L. M. (2012). *Living language: An introduction to linguistic anthropology*. New York: Wiley-Blackwell.

ComScore. (2012). Smartphone platform wars intensify as android and apple take the lead in most markets. Comscore data mine. http://www.comscoredatamine.com/2012/02/smartphone-platform-wars-intensify-as-android-and-apple-take-the-lead-in-most-markets/. Accessed Jan 2014.

Garret, J. J. (2009). The memphis plenary. http://www.jjg.net/ia/memphis/. Accessed Jan 2014.

Geertz, C. (1973). *The interpretation of cultures*. New York: Basic Books.

Geertz, C. (1983). *Local knowledge: Further essays in interpretive anthropology*. New York: Basic Books.

Hall, E. T. (1966). *The hidden dimension*. New York: Doubleday.

Hall, E. T. (1976). *Beyond culture*. New York: Doubleday.

Handwerker, W. P. (2001). *Quick ethnography*. AltaMira Press, Lanham, MA.

Hinton, A. (2008). Linkosophy. http://www.inkblurt.com/2008/04/15/linkosophy/. Accessed Jan 2014.

Kitchin, R., & Dodge, M. (2011). *Code/space-software and everyday life*. Cambridge: MIT Press.

Klyn, D. (2010). Explaining information architecture. http://wildlyappropriate.com/2010/01/20/explaining-information-architecture/. Accessed Jan 2014.

Kottak, C. P. (2012). *Window on humanity: A concise introduction to anthropology* (5th ed.). New York: McGraw Hill.

Miller, D., & Horst, H. A. (2012). The digital and the human: A prospectus for digital anthropology. In H. A. Horst & D. Miller (Eds.) *Digital anthropology*. Oxford: Berg.

Pew Research Center. (2013). Trend data (adults): Device ownership. Pew internet & American life project. http://www.pewinternet.org/Static-Pages/Trend-Data-(Adults)/Device-Ownership.aspx. Accessed Jan 2014.

Resmini, A., & Rosati, L. (2009). Information architecture for ubiquitous ecologies. *Proceedings of the International Conference on Management of Emergent Digital Ecosystems-ACM MEDES 09*. http://dx.doi.org/10.1145/1643823.1643859.

Resmini, A., & Rosati, L. (2011). *Pervasive information architecture-designing cross-channel user experiences*. San Mateo: Morgan Kaufmann.

Rosenfeld, L., & Morville, P. (1998). *Information architecture for the world wide web* (1st ed.). Cambridge: O'Reilly.

Society for Linguistic Anthropology. (2014). About the society for linguistic anthropology. http://linguisticanthropology.org/about/. Accessed Jan 2014.

Spradley, J. P. (1970). *You owe yourself a drunk: An ethnography of urban nomads*. New York: Little, Brown and Company.

Spradley, J. P. (1979). *The ethnographic interview*. Belmont: Wadsworth.

Spradley, J. P. (1980). *Participant observation*. Belmont: Wadsworth.

Chapter 7
Toward a Semiotics of Digital Places

Roberto Maggi

Abstract Information architecture is an applied art that solves the "problems arising when we need to manage, produce and consume large amount of information"
(Resmini, Problemi dell'Informazione, 38:63–76, Resmini 2013). Information architecture reflects upon complex systems of signs, understanding their mutual relationships and finding the best way to organize them. This chapter introduces a number
of theoretical tools from semiotics that are relevant for information architecture, in
particular for tracing cultural phenomena down to the specific information architectures of specific digital places, and reflects upon the role of information architecture
in the creation of a sense of place in digital space. A definition of digital place and
of the forces acting upon it is offered, extended to cross-channel ecosystems, and
then applied to understand the way we inhabit platforms such as Facebook and
Twitter. Key factors in the creation of place information architecture impacts upon
are subsequently introduced, and then a few conclusive remarks close the chapter.

7.1 What Is a Digital Place?

The term *place*, as a linguistic first, usually indicates a limited area that stands in
opposition to the wide unlimited area that is *space*.

In humanistic geography, space is the wide open and continuous area of action
that individuals understand by experiencing movement, while place is a discrete
space devoted to the ideas of staying, resting, and engagement, aspects that all relate to "value" and a "sense of belonging", what Yi-Fu Tuan called *topophilia*, "the
affective bond between people and places" (Tuan 1974, p. 4). A place is where a
person dwells, independently from scale (e.g. Central Park or my favorite chair in
the living room). As cultural geographers argue, the bond between an individual
and a place can also be partly or totally influenced by the surrounding socio-cultural
forces (Cresswell 2004).

On the other hand, the phenomenological approach of scholars such as architect Christian Norberg-Schultz frames places as the settlements where man gathers,

R. Maggi (✉)
PoiStory, Bologna, Italy
e-mail: rob.maggi@gmail.com

A. Resmini (ed.), *Reframing Information Architecture,* Human-Computer Interaction Series,   85
DOI 10.1007/978-3-319-06492-5_7, © Springer International Publishing Switzerland 2014

tames and reproduces the natural forces of the surrounding world—gravity, the cycles of the sun—"freeing meaning from the immediate situation and making it cultural" (Norberg-Schultz 1979, p. 17). According to Norberg-Schultz the creation of an artificial place gives birth to a specific *genius loci*, a spirit of the site, and one people have to deal with in order to fully experience the essence of that place.

Although place can be socio-culturally influenced and intentionally designed by an instance of power, the way we interpret it is however extremely subjective (Lynch 1960) and influenced by specific navigational needs. Knowledge about a place is the result of the merging of multiple everyday experiences.

7.2 Semiotics of Places and Culture

If we want to explain the *sense* of a particular place—and understand the sense of that particular kind of places based on information that we call *digital*—we need to find a way to systematically analyze the way people interpret it. Here is where semiotics comes into play.

While other analytical disciplines usually separate what is in the realm of facts and what is representation, semiotics finds its own specificity in a third realm made of pure relational elements, called *interpretants* in Peirce's framework, *values* in de Saussure's, *classes* in Hjelmslev's.

These constitute the basis on which the identities of all elements pertaining to a specific system can be defined. For example, the meaning of a word depends on the difference between that particular word and the other words of that language, that is, on the *value* that word assumes within the system: its meaning does not depend on how the word sounds nor on ideas it recalls (de Saussure 1922), it is purely semiotic.

This is also why spatiality interests semiotics: through the construction of places collectivities tell what they are. They express and represent their values, which social interactions are acceptable and which are inappropriate, how do individuals should express their identities. This process is for both their own and other groups' benefit.

In semiotics, to study a place means to think of it as a text, as something that talks about something different from itself (Hammad 2003), identifying first which elements are the expression of which content, in order to delineate the two plans that compose any sign relation and delimit that particular spatial system. Topological semiotics (Greimas 1976; Marrone 2001; Hammad 2003) considers the expression plan the result of the interpretation—through several topological/gestaltic categories[1]—of the scene being perceived. The content plan would consist instead of the narrative programs inscribed within the place-text, namely the actions that can be

---

[1] For example continuous/discontinuous, internal/external, open/closed, center/periphery. These possess a corresponding culturally-influenced basic meaning, for example in Western cultures the opposition "top vs bottom" is often associated to the opposition "sacred vs profane", "internal vs external" to "secure vs dangerous".

performed within it, including all cognitive, pragmatic and emotional modalizations acting on subjects, and the cultural values that the whole place-text implies. The meaning of a place is then equivalent to "the effective actions it produces on the subjects who get in touch with it" (Marrone 2001, p. 322).

However, semiotics also considers perception to be highly intertwined with an individual's goals in a particular context, and massively influenced by her previous experiences and knowledge. For example, the presence of other people moving within a scene can lead me to focus on particular elements and influence my interpretation. Then, what elements are in and what are outside of "place" when considered as a formal object?

When we *interpret* a place—as well as a sign in general—we don't merely *associate* a preexistent set of perceived elements with something else that is not present but still prefabricated (an idea, a concept). Indeed, the expression plan and the content plan of a sign are *the result* of the particular interpretation act we perform when conferring sense to that sign (Paolucci 2010, pp. 337–372). The first step of every interpretation is, in fact, to decide a so called "encyclopedic plan of pertinence", a structured group of cultural units acting as a background that allows us to suppose that a specific "sign function" is in action. Then, while proceeding through the interpretation act, hypotheses can be rearranged, proved, or corrected until we get to a valid interpretation (at least, valid for us)[2]. Therefore, to define a place as a text we need *to get out of it* and take into account also other "texts, speeches, sedimented representations, social practices, paths" (Violi 2009, p. 117) and all cultural elements that contribute to the overall meaning of that place.

Culture functions like an organism, where each part—every text, every social practice—lives in such close correlation with the others that a change in one single element modifies the whole semiotic system that element belongs to (Lotman 1985), in a substantial isomorphism. Furthermore, culture works by elaborating and handing down content, both synchronously—through communication—and asynchronously—through memory. Any society creates several coherent representations of itself as means to control its own functioning: these representations actually act as *self-models*, representations with specific goals that can be grouped in three classes (Lotman and Uspenskij 1975):

a. *self-models that reproduce reality,* that aim at telling facts congruently. For example, an official encyclopedic entry;
b. *self-models that are distant from reality,* and that aim at changing reality. For example, a religious practice that teaches compassion;
c. *self-models that work as ideal self-consciousness,* utopian and unattainable. For example, the idea of a "pure art" not influenced by a sub-culture.

Places have a primary role in this framework not only because they are cultural texts, but especially because they are environments that allow social practices to be performed, eventually becoming self-models that frame the behaviors of those

---

[2] This point of view is supported by most semioticians, especially those who refer to the interpretative semiotics approach and Eco. For more on this and the opposing views of generative semiotics, see References.

who participate. As a matter of fact, any practice consists of a certain interaction that happens in a certain place: whether it is among people or between people and objects, a practice consists of certain activities performed in one or more settings through the concrete presence of people and/or objects (or their so called simulacral form).

How should we deal then with the relationships between a place and the cultural practices it allows? We should always try to collocate a place *within* the cultural dynamics of which it is part, by setting up *series* of significant objects (Foucault 1969; Lorusso 2010). Every place is a cultural organ in the body of society dedicated to certain socio-cultural interactions.

7.3   The Forces of Digital Space and the Hodological Turn

"We live online". It is a common turn of phrase, and it implies a series of nontrivial facts, including the idea that *the digital is a space,* and not simply a medium. Indeed, the digital world we know is *navigable,* and by interacting with it we understand its spatial dynamics: a gesture in digital space corresponds to a topological change (Murray 2012); the organization of its areas is meaningful and reflective of orders and pertinences; maps can be created that represent the relationships between its elements.

There are forces as well, underlying this digital habitability—analogous to gravity or the sun's cycles: its algorithmic nature; multilinearity; componibility; the possibility to be acted upon; freedom from material support.

Algorithmic Nature Digital space is based on calculus and in plenty of "good compromise(s)" to transition out of analog without much loss (Lanier 2010). Since new media, including digital spaces, is "created on computers, distributed via computers, and stored and archived on computers, the logic of a computer can be expected to significantly influence the traditional cultural logic of media" (Manovich 2001, p. 46). And while every algorithm, however complex, is mathematically defined and its unpredictability will fall short of the complexity of the "natural" world, it is still complexity that we ordinarily cannot manage. This makes it equivalent to an inspiring natural force, just like the laws of physics or gravity.

Multilinearity At the heart of digital space there is hypertextuality, what Ted Nelson defined simply as "non-sequential writing" (Nelson 1992). This means that every text in digital space provides an inversion between paradigm and syntagm (Manovich 2001, pp. 229–233): if linearity consists in an implicit paradigm entailed by the sequential nature of the syntagm, here the paradigm is made explicit and the user determines the text's syntagm through her actions[3]. These free-access

---

[3] This dynamic is also at the basis of Kirby's idea of pseudo-modernism: "what is central now is the busy, active, forging work of the individual who would once have been called its recipient" (Kirby 2006).

alternatives allow us to follow different directions, to retrace our steps, to skip some parts or run through the same paths again at will[4].

Componibility Hypertextuality allows to compose any number of separate objects into one single artifact. Every digital space can become a fragment of another digital space through an operation that decontextualizes it and reconfigures a part of its expression plan and of its content plan, factually changing the sign function in action. It is a semiotic movement of meanings that produces new navigable spaces.

Possibility to be Acted Upon Unlike analogical spaces, digital spaces constitutively imply the possibility to be acted upon. A forest can evolve over centuries without any implications of action on the part of human beings, but every fragment of digital space entails an active human presence.

Freedom from Material Support Since digital spaces are made of bits, they can be reallocated at will on different supports. Still, they are not immaterial, as they need to be grounded in some material support, digital, physical, or hybrid, in order to be actionable.

These forces have consequences on the way people move and interact within digital space: the algorithmic nature and the possibility to be acted upon lead designers to create algorithmically controlled environments where individuals are encouraged to perform actions. These actions are pre-coded within the system, even those that the designers had not expected.

Indeed, like a novel or a film, digital space implements a textual strategy through affordances, clues and feedbacks to drive actors within the system to perform specific cognitive actions. This strategy implies what semiotics calls a model reader (Eco 1979), namely the requirements a reader must fulfil to actualize the text's potential content: the reader indeed interprets the text on the basis of what it allows her to do (*intentio operis*), independently of the will of the empirical author (*intentio auctoris*).

Eco's theory of textual cooperation is a helpful framework: movement within a digital space ends up being perceived as pure interpretative movement rather than bodily movement. And while liminal movements have been progressively forced to a limited set (we touch a screen with our fingertips), cognitive actions in digital space and occurring through semiotic interpretative mechanisms have increased. It is important to remember that digital spaces do not need to be represented in 3D. As Murray (2012) noted, it is possible to move within verbally narrated spaces as in the early text adventure game Zork. Spatiality concerns the comprehension of topological relationships and is not grounded in a specific substance or support: its visual representation is nothing but one possible *interpretant* of it—in Peirce's terminology—a sign that stands for that space in one specific respect. This also introduces the important corollary that when computing becomes ubiquitous through mobile devices, kiosks, real-time displays, and sensors, each of these touchpoints

---

[4] At every moment of its existence, the electronic text consists in several alternative virtual paths, which become actualized when the branches appears, and only one of them becomes realized after a choice is made (Zinna 2008).

becomes an entry point into digital spatiality, effectively creating the overlapping layer of cyberspace mentioned by Resmini and Rosati (2011).

Since movement within this fluid, complex and pervasive space is not bodily-based but has a strong cognitive connotation, how can we explain and study the act of dwelling in the digital? We need one more piece for this specific puzzle: Bollnow and his theory of space that frames spatiality as anthropological and not physical/ mathematical in nature (1963). Bollnow insists that space is relative, depending upon individual, direct and personal experience. In his approach, all spatial references happen relative to a subjective system that is articulated through the focal points of an individual navigation: where we start from, and where we return. Our own house, or a hotel room when on holidays. These focal points continuously change and every new step reconfigures space in dynamic "sacred-safe" areas that we consider familiar and "profane-hostile" areas where chaos reigns. This is what Bollnow calls "hodological space", a space of movement,

> based on the factual topological, physical, social, and psychological conditions a person is faced with on the way from point A to point B (Ergenter 1992).

Space is paths and experiences along these paths and "corresponds exactly to what we perceive if we move between two different locations" (Resmini and Rosati 2011, p. 68).

Safe, in a hodological sense, is what is familiar, the units that are part of our cultural knowledge. Hostile spaces are characterized by breadth, strangeness, and distance (Bollnow 1961, pp. 4–5). *Breadth* is the absence of restrictions that attracts us, but also deprives us of all stable points and of the security to both control the world and control ourselves. *Strangeness*, instead, is what makes us feel helpless, because what we experience follows rules that we have never encountered. *Distance* is the difference between that particular space and what is "our own", a gap that seduces us by showing an organization different from our habits, a difference that exhorts us to go beyond what we know.

The act of moving through the space is therefore just a continuous act of re-interpreting as safe or as hostile what surrounds us. Streets become networks, a safe way to move into the world and an accepted habit in Western commons sense. What lies beyond the streets is experienced from the vantage point of the "safe way":

> The motorist does not move in the surrounding country, but just on the road, and remains separated from the country by a sharp boundary. The countryside becomes a panorama which passes by (…) He can enjoy its beauty, but it is remote as a picture. His real feeling of space is that of breadth and of the speed which opens up broad spaces. This is the space he lives, his real space, not the picturesque view (Bollnow 1961, p. 5).

Like the motorist's, our exploration of digital space moves first of all along the trails drawn by others, trails that cross the information universe following schemes that become conventional over time. From a semiotic perspective these schemes are organs of the bigger organism of culture: as such, we learn how to move within digital space by observing the behaviors of the social groups we get in touch with, and by following the movement schemes they are used to.

7.4 The Digital Place and Its Genius Loci

How can we now define what is a digital *place*?

What we are dealing with is a complex and heterogeneous space, a hostile chaos that must somehow be understood and tamed. Manovich describes it through the analogy of the database, a model that "represents the world as a list of items, and (...) refuses to order this list" (Manovich 2001, p. 225), leaving to the user the burden of choosing among the paradigmatic alternatives, as opposed to the "cause-and-effect trajectory" among elements generated when we are in presence of a *narrative*. The opposition "database vs narrative" is not just a question of "order vs disorder", but is primarily a question of *safe streets* through which we make sense of the hostile information overload.

Therefore granting easy access to information is certainly important, but creating *a narrative set up of the pathway* is paramount. An information space where we feel safe is one that *tells* a world and does not limit itself to expressing it: it sets itself up in order to house us as individuals within it, it suggests how to move, it makes our actions easier and, above all, it causes us (good or bad) emotional reactions at each step.

Narrative is articulated through three components: an *actantial structure*, that defines narrative roles which then, at the discourse level, become characters who have specific thematic roles[5]; a procedure of *aspectualization*—divided in temporalization, actorialization (character marks) and spatialization, that on the whole express the observer's perspective on the discourse—and that manifest the actantial structure at the discursive level; a process of *modalization* of individuals at the cognitive, pragmatic and passional level, which acts as the main narrative engine. Every action is the consequence of a relational and tensive structure[6].

If we apply this framing to digital space, for example that of a social network, it results that we feel comfortable there because its space *talks about us*, not in the sense that it allows us to talk about ourselves, but because *it includes us as subjects and confers us a role in a story*. It tells us that we have the opportunity to change the development of a story and, exactly like in a videogame, it shows the result of every actions we perform by inscribing it in its space. Thus, the narrative set-up makes us feel at home and creates a microcosm wherein it is possible to dwell. Narration *per se* seems to be the theoretical core that allows us to identify a digital place.

Narration and place are indeed connected. A story expresses a specific topology: it has places for events to happen and it must create a spatial location for each role and every narrative program that it articulates explicitly. On the other hand, it is place that makes a story possible, and in digital places discorsive aspectualization

---

[5] Narrative roles differ from thematic roles. For example, Snowwhite is a child (thematic role) who is the subject (narrative role) of the story, and the seven dwarves (thematic roles) act as her helper (as a single narrative role).

[6] For an introductory overview on the process of modalization, see Greimas and Courtés 1979, p. 209.

is mainly a spatial aspectualization[7]. Thus, a digital place is a *spatial striature* (Deleuze and Guattari 1980) that implies and suggests the pathways to cross it and escape from it, encouraging individuals to let these possibilities of action seduce them, and to live the story it exposes. Indeed, the "modal weight" of the role that an individual plays in the story can influence her actions only after a cognitive modalization, that is, only when she "wants-to-do" or "has-to-do" something.

Digital places are not cohesive, closed structures. The cultural network is what influences the relationship between individuals and places. If a digital place is indeed a place, it is because we can take part to certain social practices within it, practices that are only meaningful within the social context we live. What conditions us is the rigidity of the behavioral rules these practices follow: accepting or refusing them is something that exceeds any specific place-text, and has to do with the interpretative practices that a collectivity shares.

For example, we could choose to take revenge of an overly finicky boss making fun of her on Facebook. The technology-mediated physical distance between us and her makes some of the behavioral rules of the analogical world feel less imposing. Similarly, we use Facebook more and more to congratulate friends on their birthday because posting our wishes there charges the action with more meaning and emotional content. Maybe we share a picture. This interaction between analogical and digital practices is one of the most interesting aspect of this problem space, as it invisibly changes the *common sense*, "not what the mind cleared of cant spontaneously apprehends (but) what the mind filled with presuppositions concludes" (Geertz 1983).

Considering a digital place in terms of narration means considering it as a textual manifestation of a narration. The website or mobile app *can be* a digital place when it textualizes one or several existing *visiting practices* and *dwelling practices*. Indeed, every website sets itself and the individual visitors up as *actants* of a narrative and does a certain *mise-en-discourse* of several specific narrative programs. However, while every website instantiates some visiting practices—articulated through viewing, searching and selection pathways—we can dwell just in a few of them[8].

However, considering digital places in terms of narration does not entail that a website or an app *is* a digital place. Digital spatiality is pervasive and thinking in terms of isolated, independent websites has little sense. In the connected world of today, individuals interact with a certain entity—be it another individual, group of peers, band, book, company, institution, topic, or event—through a plethora of different channels that allow access to the same (or parts of the same) narration, where

---

[7] "Me" is present in the scene in all different semiotic modes of existence—virtual, actual, and real—thanks to input-boxes, buttons, images and icons; others are present to this "me" through their pictures and texts, positions convey meaning, and temporal flow is articulated through specific ordering/linking of content.

[8] In the mid-1990s we could navigate the Internet but we could only dwell in our electronic mailboxes, the one space that we could consider our own. The rest of the time we were just passing through, visiting, observing, understanding, extending our cultural knowledge, accumulating pictures of the surrounding landscape, but ultimately moving elsewhere.

we have the same role in the story and we can perform, although in different ways, the same narrative programs.

It is the complex ecosystem that includes the website and the app that manifests a digital place, not the single channel nor the sum of them. If this ecosystem requires an individual to interact with physical artifacts as well, then the digital place includes these as well. For example, the narration that takes place in the digital place "Sant'Orsola Malpighi", a hospital located in Bologna, Italy, includes the way-finding signage within the compound, a website, a mobile app, patient and staff experiences reported on a trade magazine, conversations on social media, and in-hospital systems. Narration cannot be reduced to reside in any single artifact: it naturally spans across all of these channels (Resmini and Rosati 2011).

According to Murray (2012), when I live a first-person experience within a virtual space—experience related to me as individual and not to my avatar—I accept the reality of that world and identify myself with my digital self. Therefore, the notion of digital place can be defined as a limited area of digital space, with a name and a stable if fleeting identity, that embeds us as actants of a story articulated through a pervasive information architecture (with a specific amount of pervasiveness) across different channels, that confers us a role and that defines the grammar for those practices of interaction we can take part to.

7.5   Semiotics for Information Architecture

Let us now apply this semiotics-oriented theoretical framework to Facebook and Twitter, to understand how they respectively construct the identity of their users and their social interactions. I will try to analyze how these systems confer a thematic role to us and how they include us in the narrative they create. Pages, tools, widgets, connections, hyperlinks, these compose the scene that we need to investigate, and from our analytic perspective they are the discorsive manifestations of the narrative structures in place[9].

Facebook and Twitter have at least three formal traits in common:

- they both allow people to aggregate with individuals that are far beyond the reach of their physical social network—this implies that both systems have a specific idea of what is one's "real" social network—parents, relatives, colleagues, close friends—and how to extend it;
- they both have at least two dimensions through which individuals can express their identities: the *synchronic dimension*—namely a representation of the self that seldom changes, and that constitutes a core group of information with which an individual can self-identify, such as a name, short bio, and profile pic—and

---

[9] These are presented as introductory case studies and not as a complete analysis of a vast cultural phenomenon, for which two items only are certainly not an appropriate series. Also consider that the analysis takes into account the Italian cultural semiosphere. Some aspects might work differently—or be not pertinent—in other cultures.

the *diachronic dimension*—namely the content being posted over time, having the peculiarity of becoming a log of that person's evolution;
• they both construct identity and social interactions along three axes: *self-telling*, ways and mechanisms to tell one's story for both personal and public benefit; *pervasiveness*, ways and mechanisms to link a real identity to the one represented in the digital world; and *intersubjectivity*, ways and mechanisms to represent and expose the relationships between an individual and others.

We need to keep in mind that when an individual starts using one of (or both) these platforms she usually reduces the time she dedicates to other customary socio-cultural activities. This thoroughly reorganizes the value she attributes to every single activity she performs daily.

7.6 Facebook and the College-Identity Stereotype

To understand how Facebook constructs our identity, we need to observe the elements related to the task of representing ourselves and those related to the process of viewing content.

In Facebook, the former relate to what can be called the *exhibitionist narrative program,* which proceeds through the insertion of biographic information, the posting of content, and the performing of social actions such as shares or likes. Facebook works through stereotypical characteristics (movies we like, places we visit), emphasizing the traits that make us similar to what the system already knows. In the 90's, as well as in the early versions of MySpace, identity could be expressed any way we liked, posting all of the information *we* believed was important about us on blank slate webpages.

Instead, Facebook does not only ask us to precisely declare some indicators (for example, our workplace) and not others (for example, our favorite dish or film director), but often structures choices via lists of preexisting elements and sometimes forces us to choose anyway, as with the infamous relationship entry.

From a narrative point of view, this means that if we find an adequate element to describe ourselves in the list we are positively sanctioned by the system, whereas if we cannot find any we perceive our behavior or status as not appropriate in respect to the place "normality". *To be* on Facebook means to flatten out our personality to the stereotypical person template available on the platform: whoever is not willing to do this will not fully get in tune with the place and its genius loci.

This is confirmed at the discursive level, where the synchronic profile information is shown through a largely static layout that has been already chosen for us. Semiotically, adding my information and organizing it in a page is a particular interpretation of the object "identity". In the 1990s, both the point of view[10] and the

---

[10] In semiotics, the point of view is "a set of procedures utilized by the enunciator in order to (...) diversify the reading which the enunciatee will make of the narrative" (Greimas and Courtés 1979, pp. 237–238). We discern the different points of view of the policeman and the robber, regardless

discourse perspective were the user's[11]: Facebook limited both the point of view and the perspective: our profile page, as a place, does not talk about our identity, but rather about the particular interpretation that Facebook wants to make of it.

The diachronic dimension of identity is instead articulated through two processes: posting content, and liking or sharing social objects[12]. The design principles behind these are the same we noted for the synchronic dimension. When we post something we are forced to choose a type of content, and the more specialized the content type is (for example, life events), the more the system will reward us with a visually distinctive sign of our personality on the timeline. We are led to reduce our activities to a set of standardized representations. And when we click on the *like* button—whose semantic is not articulated through a "positive vs negative" opposition but is factually equivalent to conferring a vote that can only be revoked via *un*-liking—we are reducing our affective bond to the simplified, fan-like logic of digital.

If the exhibitionist paths are evident, those of the *voyeuristic narrative program*—related to the process of viewing—are hidden and embedded in the place's *mise en scène*. Facebook constructs us as observers, and confers us a "want-to-watch" trait that is constitutive of our act of dwelling in this place. While we scroll the viewport, the interface keeps us focused on our value-object—content—by hiding, excluding or moving the remaining elements, driving our voyeurism to a climax.

All the same, the place is structured to maintain several references to us in view (profile picture, notification bar), making it clear that this area does not talk about us but it includes us as an actant of the narrative.

Through its architecture, Facebook teaches us how to move our attention quickly from a piece of content to another, implying that this is the correct way to act to fully live up to its potentiality. In response, we develop a behavioral habit that shortens the amount of time we consider necessary to understand an event. Basically, the voyeuristic narrative program trains us so that we can stay on Facebook all of the time and reduce the time/depth of our thinking and engage in a parody of American college life.

7.7 Interaction, Reputation and Beyond

To be coherent with the American college semantic isotopy, the base model of activity consists in a post followed by a judgment (the number of likes and shares) and a series of comments. As soon as I post something, say a picture, it goes on to occupy a slot in the stream and it appears on my "friends" timelines, who are included as participants in what is already an actualized conversation. To a friend, my post

---

of who is recounting the facts: emphasizing carefully chosen facets of "identity" at the expense of others modifies the point of view on identity itself.

[11] For example, compare the rigid predetermination offered by Facebook to the freedom and flexibility of earlier platforms such as MySpace.

[12] Joining groups or events works similarly.

is represented with two additional links—"Like" and "Comment"—that mark her potential presence and modalize her both with a "be-able-to-comment" and "know-how-to-comment", entailing that she *has the right* to comment.

An interesting aspect of this social architecture is the fact that moderation—the deletion of undesired comments—is possible just *a posteriori*, after the comment has had its role into the discussion. For those who particularly care about what other people say about their posts, this aspect creates another narrative program, tasked with the *obsessive control of reputation*. This mechanism is present in different ways in all social platforms, and many of them—Twitter for example—do not allow deleting an undesired reply by another user. As a consequence, digital space has silently introduced the cultural practice of the *unavoidable dialogue* as a form of weak control system: if you aim to have a conversation that can positively promote your content/brand, then you will have to lead the discussion where you want it to go and deal with consequences, including undesired criticism.

If the strategy is simply to delete what is not in line with the desired narrative, people will notice and will react consequently. The only way to moderate successfully entails engaging others in constructive dialogue—and this is why companies or politicians have their "brand reputation" managed 24/24 by dedicated professionals.

A thorough awareness of the social dynamics of the digital place is also necessary: in 2011, then Italian Prime Minister Mario Monti (or someone from his staff) demonstrated a complete lack of understanding posting on Facebook that "(m)aking proposals is acceptable, but insulting is not. We remind you, if it is needed, that offences posted on this social network site—as in every other place—could be prosecuted." Analog politics enters a place whose architecture is designed to go beyond real-life social hierarchies, a place that models the interactions between us and the Prime Minister in the same way it models the interactions between us and our friends or siblings, and completely misses the cue.

The model "post+comments" is also at the base of Facebook's *groups*. Groups are used by people to aggregate around topics of interest, and derive from the forum model. While in analog life joining a group requires effort to keep up-to-date and participate, on Facebook the system keeps us informed at every changes in the stream. This has an interesting effect, for example, in the way students participate in protests: in a study about the use of digital tools in the widespread protest against the educational reform in Italy 2008–2012, Capelli and Fiocchi (2009) demonstrated that *borderline* students "who support the protest movement but do not want to go the full mile" are attracted to join the Facebook groups "because of the weaker relationship it requires" compared to joining the militant mailing-lists. Clicking "Like" or sharing posts is what they do to support the cause: the story Facebook is telling is that this way they have an active role nonetheless.

Cultural values are flattened as well: in the analog world the practice of joining a protest and the practice of joining a group to organize a film festival are considered very different things, but the digital side of those practices on Facebook is the same: joining a group, clicking on "Like", commenting and sharing information with friends. Socio-cultural practices as diverse as exchanging notes about university classes or arguing over a pop star meltdown are reduced, through a common information architecture, to the same practice.

7.8 Twitter and Identities on the Go

Twitter's idea of identity is instead characterized by minimalism in both the synchronic and diachronic dimensions.

Profiles allow for a short description of oneself, shorter than Facebook, but this does not mean that personality is not important, it is just expressed differently. Twitter tells us "let your tweets talk about you". This way Twitter constructs an *individual on the go* who lives her experiences and shares them in almost real-time, who describes events as a witness.

On one side, we are our authentic and sincere self, "not-able-not-to-communicate" emotions; on the other hand, we are "on-task", interpreting and signifying what we perceive, mediating the world. The temporal aspectualization—realized through the chronological ordering of tweets, the timestamps, and the adoption of specific verbal tenses when tweeting—produces an effect of sense that leads us to believe in an effective equivalence between what is posted and what is happening: that tweet is the real emotional status of that person at that moment. Geo-location often contributes to extend the pervasiveness of the digital place to the analog world, anchoring it across channels[13].

A Twitter identity is also by and large *public*. There is no explicit notion of "private" visibility over what we can post, nor an explicit subdivision in friends' lists that receive different sets of message (such as Facebook's lists or Google+ circles). Followers are granted rights to read any of our tweets with the exception of direct messages, one on one conversations that Twitter has been trying to downplay for quite a while. Twitter constructs us as worthy to be listened to, owner of a "be-able-to-be" that sets all of us on the same level of social importance. This influences our pragmatic acting, because it implies a series of cultural limits: we feel we have the same influence than those who occupy positions in society we might consider more important and this leads us to build our diachronic identity following specific narrative programs coded in the architecture.

A first narrative entails the role of *know-it-all*: since the place confers me the right to easily intervene in every conversation, I feel it's my right to do so, and I take on the role of news reporter, commentator, politician, expert of new media, chef extraordinaire. The positive sanction coming from the fact that I am part of the discussion—and that my tweets will remain in the discussion log with the same visual weight of every other opinion—increases the effect of sense that leads me to

---

[13] Note Twitter's freedom from material support: the command set still works today through SMS and it is entirely possible to change one's profile description (SET BIO <text>), send a direct message, or poke someone entirely via text messages.

confer correctness and relevance to what I am posting, especially when my tweet is shared through retweets.

The second narrative program is driven by *discretion*: as everybody will see my tweet, my words carry weight. As a beginner tweeter, my tweeting is poor and I fear being scrutinized. The panoptical nature of the place's architecture weighs on me[14]; as I improve, my posts will begin to be edited to support the narrative I'm weaving. As Francis Bacon would say, it seems that those 140 characters are not a blank space to be filled in, but a canvas bulging out with all our cultural suppositions.

Obviously, nobody follows one of these narrative programs strictly: there is always a degree of blending that makes our digital presence more human-like and informal. Even so, we can observe a *uniforming regularity,* analogous to Facebook's standardizing tendency, especially visible when events are live-tweeted. During these marathons, a high percentage of the tweets are just transcripts of a catchy phrase being said, implying a lack of re-interpretation that results in a conflation of our diachronic identity to someone else's.

Furthermore, by conferring us the role of "follower", Twitter modalizes us with a "wanting-to-know" that drives all our narrative programs of discovery, with the value-object here being any piece of information about the world that another user could provide us with, instead of information about that user[15].

7.9   Looking for Context

Twitter's architecture of social interactions sees no opposition between an author and those who contribute with comments, but rather frames a debate among same-level speakers that reply to each other. Linguistically, the lexemes "to comment" and "to reply" activate two different semantic frames: a comment expresses the sender's opinion on a subject, opinion that could exist independently from a debate; a reply, on the other hand, entails a *dialectic* between two or more people in reference to a specific discussion.

The Twitter and Facebook models are very different. It is clearly possible to use Facebook's commenting tools to debate, and use Twitter's replies to comment, but the spatial setup of a Facebook interaction always represents a visual hierarchy that sees the main content top, in a larger area, and with a larger font size in respect to replies in the thread. This is not the case in Twitter, where messages are showed independently and indicate their status as part of a conversation with special icons

---

[14] For an excellent, Foucault-inspired discussion of how our lives are turning into "lives in a digital panopticon", see Rayner (2012).

[15] Interestingly enough, pictures have never be at the center of the Twitter publishing system, contrary to what happens on Facebook, where the use of pictures is supported as a best practice. In 2011, the Twitter user interface—both the website and its mobile counterparts—showed every image as a link within the text. As of 2013 this has changed, but the layout still renders text before any picture, preserving the design principle that textual content lies at the core of the Twitter experience.

and links. There is no *a priori* "wanting-to-do": in order to participate, we need to actively decide to access the thread, and even then, conversations remain difficult to follow as they unfold non-linearly and the lack of an always visible representation grouping the messages increases both the dispersion of information and the cognitive load for late-in-the-game readers.

This lack of context has always been a Twitter issue, and it was worse early on when no mechanism was in place to connect tweets. Several proposals to aggregate tweets by subject or thread were discussed, and ultimately the *hashtag* proposed by Chris Messina was chosen. The now familiar syntax "*# + keyword*" derives from the language of late 1980s IRC chatrooms, a way to associate all messages from users that join a specific conversation space, so that a group is generated and preserved over time. However, Messina was not suggesting groups, but rather trying to help users understand the *context* of an ongoing conversation:

> Every time someone uses a *channel tag* to mark a status, not only do we know something specific about that status, but others can eavesdrop on the context of it and then join in the channel and contribute as well. Rather than trying to ping-pong discussion between one or more individuals (Messina 2007).

Hashtags allow Twitter digital places to expand beyond the physical boundaries of a socio-cultural practice: a conference is enriched by a digital layer constituted *in primis* by the presence of people who declare to be part of that story by using its specific hashtag.

7.10   Conclusions

Digital spatiality is characterized by five traits that we have called its *algorithmic nature, multilinearity, componibility, possibility to be acted upon,* and *freedom from material support*. Information architects gather and ply these forces to build digital places and allow people to dwell in them by including them as actants in a story, conferring specific roles to them, and designing the socio-cultural practices they can take part in.

I maintained that in respect to this framework, services such as Facebook or Twitter configure places, and I proceeded to examine the way these two construct identities and interaction mechanisms through the three perspective axes of *self-telling, pervasiveness* and *intersubjectivity*.

The exploration of both their impact on society and the way they have progressively substituted "being here" with dwelling in a place that is not bounded by the rules of analogical space forces us to reflect on one of the most interesting questions being debated today: if—or how much—what is digital is real[16].

What I proposed here is that we frame this opposition, *digital vs real*, as a dialogue between two different cultures, two different semiospheres. A semiosphere

---

[16] "Digital is real" was the theme for the Italian Information Architecture Conference 2013.

has a so called "semiotic personality", constituted by texts and practices, and grows through progressive exchanges with different cultures, creating "through its own efforts this «alien» that brings a different consciousness, that codes the texts and the world in different ways" (Lotman 1985, p. 124). This allows for the translation of anomalies into comprehensible normalities, but, as Lotman notes,

> the introduction of alien cultural structures in the inner world of a culture involves the creation of a common language and this, in turn, requires the interiorisation of those structures. Therefore, a culture has to interiorise the alien culture inside its world (Lotman 1985).

Over the last twenty years and more, analogical and digital culture have conducted exactly this kind of dialogue, opposing and exchanging their different social structures, the articulation of personal and collective identities, their socio-cultural practices, the very idea of being here or there in space. This mutual translation between the two semiospheres created an *upper level semiosphere* where the articulation of socio-cultural phenomena is hybrid and merges what is digital with what is analogical, turning this new blend into the *de facto* "real". This process is far from being over: the increasing amount of time we spend "online" steadily raises the impact architecting the digital has in shaping society, while the importance of analogical-only structures of culture keeps decreasing.

Information architecture is a primary contributor to the shaping of this dialogue between the digital and the real: information architects build digital places that will become self-models for the society of tomorrow. As such, information architecture has a profound impact on our social and cultural structures that is mostly expressed through its handling, good or bad, of three specific factors:

1. Digital places have the intrinsic tendency to reduce identity and social interactions to stereotypes individuals are forced to accept in order to fully dwell within the environment. This act of reducing ourselves to a social structure that is not completely equivalent to that of the analog semiosphere produces a double action/rejection mechanisms: we are seduced by its diversity, but we understand that we are being reduced. Any capability to reject this reduction is an illusion: even if we can create a fake or parallel identity, the narrative programs lead us to embrace certain behaviors in terms of content that we post and dynamics we experience. Living in a digital place implies a reduction to what its architecture wants us to be: hence, when structuring a narrative program, information architects need to be aware of what they are asking actants to be.
2. Different socio-cultural practices are equalized on the basis of an identical interaction model. Digital places lead us to overlap the cultural backgrounds pertaining to completely different practices by reducing every practice to the same structure: this way we progressively induce individuals to perceive every situation not corresponding to the model as lacking or faulty. The individual learns to interact through certain dynamics and develops a need to apply those dynamics to every aspect of life. The fact that we are comfortable with the Facebook model of interaction does not mean that that model is compatible with every socio-cultural practice: by applying it as is we would reduce every practice to

Facebook's architecture[17]. When designing an interaction mechanism to enhance any analogical socio-cultural practice, we should act like cultural mediators and respect the cultural values that that practice carries with it.

3. Digital places determine the timing of an individual's activities. Because of the sheer amount of information and the "publish then filter" model that these services adopt, to participate successfully we are forced to quickly scan content and collect as much knowledge as possible in the shortest possible time. This pushes us towards an always-on model that allows us to stay up-to-date with the events, and moves our reflections towards shallowness: to dwell in these digital places we have to follow the strict timing that their information architectures impose on us. When considering the amount of time individuals spend in our system, we should strike a balance between the needs of the actors and the requirements of the platform.

References

Bollnow, O. F. (1961). Lived space. The Otto Friedrich Bollnow society. http://www.otto-fried-rich-bollnow.de/doc/LivedSpace.pdf.

Bollnow, O. F. (1963). *Mensh und Raum*. Stuttgart: Kohlhammer.

Capelli, A., & Fiocchi, G. (2009). Facebook come un'onda. In R. Borgato, F. Capelli, & M. Ferraresi (Eds.), *Facebook come. Le nuove relazioni virtuali* (pp. 137–146). Milano: Franco Angeli.

Cresswell, T. (2004). *Place: A short introduction*. Maiden: Blackwell.

de Saussure, F. (1922). *Cours de linguistique générale*. Paris: Editions Payot.

Deleuze, G., & Guattari, F. (1980). *Mille Plateux. Capitalism et schizofrénie*. Paris: Les Éditions de Minuit.

Eco, U. (1979). *Lector in Fabula*. Milano: Bompiani.

Ergenter, N. (1992). *Otto Friedrich Bollnow's anthropological concept of space*. Proceedings of the 5th International Congress of the International Association for the Semiotic of Space. Berlin. http://home.wordcome.ch/~negenter/012BollnowE1.html.

Foucault, M. (1969). *L'archéologie du savoir*. Paris: Éditions Gallimard.

Geertz, C. (1983). *Local knowledge: Further essays in interpretative anthropology*. New York: Basic Books.

Greimas, A. J. (1976). *Pour une sémiotique topologique*. Sémiotique et sciences sociales. Paris: Seuil.

Greimas, A. J., & Courtés, J. (1979) Semiotique. Dictionnaire reisonné de la théorie du langage. Hacette. Eng. *Semiotics and Language. An Analytical Dictionary*. Blooming University Press.

Hammad, M. (2003). *Leggere lo spazio, comprendere l'architettura*. Roma: Meltemi.

Kirby, A. (2006). The death of postmodernism and beyond. *Philosophy Now,* Issue 58. http://philosophynow.org/issues/58/The_Death_of_Postmodernism_And_Beyond. Accessed January 2014.

Lanier, J. (2010). *You are not a gadget*. New York: Knopf.

Lorusso, A. M. (2010). Semiotica della cultura. Roma-Bari: Laterza.

Lotman, J. M. (1985). *La semiosfera. L'asimmetria e il dialogo nelle strutture pensanti*. Venezia: Marsilio Editori.

Lotman, J. M., & Uspenskij, B. A. (1975). *Tipologia della cultura*. Milano: Bompiani.

---

[17] For example, a project that tries to promote tourism in a region through an application with the same social architecture of Foursquare.

Lynch, K. (1960). *The image of the city*. Cambridge: MIT Press.

Maggi, R., & Resmini, A. (forthcoming). *Digital Genius Loci: Sense of place in a postdigital world*.

Manovich, L. (2001). *The language of new media*. Cambridge: MIT Press.

Marrone, G. (2001). *Corpi sociali: Processi comunicativi e semiotica del testo*. Torino: Einaudi.

Marrone, G. (2009). *Dieci tesi per uno studio semiotico della città. Appunti, osservazioni, proposte. Versus - Il senso dei luoghi*. Riflessioni e analisi semiotiche, 109–111, 11–46.

Messina, C. (2007). Groups for Twitter or a proposal for Twitter tag channels. http://factory-joe.com/blog/2007/08/25/groups-for-twitter-or-a-proposal-for-twitter-tag-channels/. Accessed Dec 2013.

Murray, J. H. (2012). Inventing the Medium: Principles of Interaction Design as a Cultural Practice. Cambridge: MIT Press.

Nelson, T. (1992). *Literary Machine 90.1. Il progetto Xanadu*. Padova: Franco Muzzio Editore.

Norberg-Schultz, C. (1979). *Genius Loci: Towards a phenomenology of architecture*. New York: Rizzoli.

Paolucci, C. (2010). *Strutturalismo e interpretazione*. Milano: Bompiani.

Rayner, T. (2012) Foucault and social media: life in a digital panopticon. Philosophy for change. http://philosophyforchange.wordpress.com/2012/06/21/foucault-and-social-media-life-in-a-virtual-panopticon/.

Resmini, A. (2013). Per una storia breve dell'architettura dell'informazione. *Problemi dell'Informazione, 1*, 63–76.

Resmini, A., & Rosati, L. (2011). *Pervasive information architecture, designing cross-channel user experiences*. Morgan Kauffman.

Tuan, Y. (1974). *Topophilia: A study of environmental perception, attitudes, and values*. Englewood Cliffs: Prentice-Hall.

Violi, M. P. (2009). Il senso del luogo. Qualche riflessione di metodo a partire da un caso specifico. In M. Leone (Ed.), *La città come testo: scritture e riscritture urbane*. Torino: Aracne.

Zinna, A. (2008). *Le interfacce degli oggetti di scrittura. Teoria del linguaggio e ipertesti*. Roma: Meltemi.

Chapter 8
What We Make When We Make Information Architecture

Andrew Hinton

Abstract This paper proposes a starting point for understanding the material of information architecture practice, by answering the question, "What are we architecting when we practice information architecture?" I propose in summary form some ideas about how information architecture's medium, information, can be usefully described in three modalities (physical, semantic, and digital), and how a full understanding of embodied cognition and affordance theory can help us connect the abstraction of language with structuring concrete, bodily experience.

8.1 Introduction

As a practicing information architect since the late 1990s, I have been preoccupied with how viscerally we experience the things and places that we make with mere language. How is it that human life can be so deeply affected by words on a page or screen? Why do we feel as if we are inhabiting actual places when we navigate, converse, and transact within structures that are made only with text, tags, and network protocols?

Some of my earliest work as a professional information architect involved creating the plans for places that existed only online, but that were just as important and impactful to the human activity of organizations as any physical building or campus would be. I saw that, not unlike the multi-user dungeons (MUDs) and BBSs I visited with my first modem in the late 1980s, the Web was also a medium for creating structures not just for organizing inventories of objects (pages, products, etc.), but for architecting places and that one architectural decision could make or break any given place's ability to succeed at fulfilling its intended purpose.

So, for years, I have been working on the hunch that digital technology has enabled us to create environments with language in a way that we could not quite do before. That somehow, information has become a kind of material we're using for a new sort of architectural work. Back in 2002, in a manifesto I participated in creating for what later became the Information Architecture Institute, we stated

A. Hinton (✉)
The Understanding Group, Ann Arbor, USA
e-mail: ah@andrewhinton.com

A. Resmini (ed.), *Reframing Information Architecture,* Human-Computer Interaction Series, 103
DOI 10.1007/978-3-319-06492-5_8, © Springer International Publishing Switzerland 2014

that "This work is an act of architecture: the structuring of raw information into shared information environments with useful, navigable form that resists entropy and reduces confusion. This is a new kind of architecture that designs structures of information rather than of bricks, wood, plastic and stone (…) People live and work in these structures, just as they live and work in their homes, offices, factories and malls. These places are not virtual: they are as real as our own minds." (Hinton 2002). These were lofty ideas, but I would have been hard pressed to back them up with any hard proof or sound theories.

Since that time, I have been ruminating on these questions; and now (at least for myself) I am figuring out some answers, in part through work on a book I am writing about how information creates and changes context. As part of that effort, I have developed what I hope to be a useful starting point for establishing what we are actually creating in our environment with the work of information architecture.

In this article I propose in summary form some ideas about how information architecture's medium, information, can be usefully described in three modalities (physical, semantic, and digital), and how a full understanding of embodied cognition and affordance theory can help us connect the abstraction of language with structuring concrete, bodily experience.

8.2   A Note on Semantic Affordance

In the last ten years, there have been a number of prior uses of the phrase "semantic affordance" in various academic areas of study, including cognitive science, linguistics, and robotics. Some of these uses are about how additional layers of meaning are involved in many physical affordances (Young 2006; Dang and Allen 2012), and some uses have to do with a theory of how language can activate understanding prior to (and complementary with) conceptual metaphor (Evans 2006).

For my purposes here, I am using the phrase in a more general sense for information architecture practice, namely for the way in which semantic information adds supplementary structure to our environment, which we comprehend in an embodied, ecologically grounded manner.

8.3   The Challenge

For over a decade, we have defined information architecture as (in part) "the structural design of shared information environments," (Information Architecture Institute 2002) yet we still lack a consensus for what we mean by that phrase. While this formulation does some work toward clarifying what information architecture might mean in the first place, it is also somewhat recursive: "structure" and "architecture" are nearly synonymous; "environment" is also an architectural term, as in "the built environment"; and of course merely repeating the word "information" brings little or no clarification. What do we mean when we say "information"? And in what way are we "architecting" it?

These questions are not merely academic or philosophical exercises. In very real, practical ways, we know that digital technology and global networks have made information more pervasive and active in all parts of our lives. Once the Internet slipped the bounds of the situated desktop computer and became something to which we have access all day, every day, through broadband wireless networks, it became a persistent layer in everything we do. We now depend on it the way we depend on things like agriculture and roads.

If information architecture is to mature as a practice, it needs a more solid theoretical framework for what it is doing in the world. Even before the explosion of pervasive connectivity, this lack of a foundation for key information architecture concepts has contributed to numerous problems:

- Circular discourse on the nature of what information architecture is and does, preventing the community of practice from defining its central domain and developing a full-fledged intellectual discipline that matures the practice (Hobbs et al. 2010).
- Relegation of information architecture practice to narrowly defined activities, methods, and deliverables such as "wireframes" which have matured little since their introduction to Web-based information architecture in the mid 1990s.
- Use of "information architecture methods" (such as card sorting) without understanding how or why they work, which can result in the misuse of those methods.
- Missing criteria for what makes one information architecture approach better than another. As Jesse James Garrett says, "until we have ways to describe the qualities of an information architecture, we won't be able to tell good information architecture from bad information architecture. All we'll ever be able to do is judge processes" (Garrett 2009).

At the center of the conundrum is the question of what information architecture is shaping. What is its material? Architecture for the built environment can point to the buildings, parks, and cityscapes that result from their practice. Industrial design can point to manufactured products. Interaction design can point to the interactive objects of digitally generated or enhanced interfaces. All of these disciplines deal in abstractions, because they all create plans for making. But at least the things that are made from the plans can be seen and touched.

Information architecture has trouble pointing to such things, since it has always been an abstract, interstitial practice concerned with not just what happens within things, but what happens between them, as Lou Rosenfeld pointed out in a 1997 interview (Champeon 1997)[1]. How does this "between-ness" translate to flesh-and-blood human experience and daily life?

Taking an embodied, phenomenological approach can help us understand how the abstractions of semantic structures function in concrete ways for human perception and cognition. But to make this connection between information and lived experience, we need to dig deeper into what we mean by *information*, and clarify what we mean by *environment*.

---

[1] "Argus' mission is to change the perception that information architecture pertains exclusively to the relationship of chunks of information within pages, as opposed to between pages". See References.

While there has been much work by leading figures in information science, linguistics, and other fields to define information, I propose that we circumvent the problems inherent to deciding on a single, orthodox *prescriptive* definition. Instead, I propose a pluralistic *descriptive* model, outlining three complementary modes in which information functions for human experience: physical, semantic, and digital.

8.4   Physical Information

It is important to start with a thorough description of this information mode, because it is the one that is most likely to be unfamiliar to design practitioners, and it forms the basis for understanding the other modes as well.

Physical information is an *ecological* mode, meaning it concerns the relationship between an organism and the organism's physical environment: rocks, mountains, streams, and trees, and even the structures of the human-made environment, such as buildings, roads, and bridges. In other words, the full *environment* and all the information it presents to a perceiver.

I base this mode largely on the work of pioneer ecological psychologist James J. Gibson. Gibson adopted the term *information* to mean the intrinsic structural clues an animal picks up from the interplay of energy with the surfaces and mediums of the environment. Animals perceive through action, and act based on what they perceive, which forms a sort of loop of cognition, where animals act, perceive, calibrate further action, perceive, and so on. This Gibson called the perception-action loop. This loop is not based on computed rules and symbols in the brain; rather, it emerges from the interplay between the whole body (including the brain) and its environmental surroundings, working together as an interdependent perceptual system.

Gibson rejected outright some fundamental assumptions upon which mainstream cognitive science was built through the mid 20th century. For example, he argued that there are no literal representations of the world in the brain, and that memory is not a singular function that can be located and fully described the way it can with something like a computer. These stances have caused Gibson's ideas to be sidelined for many years in conventional cognitive theory circles. (Wilson 2011). However, in recent years, Gibson's ecological approach has been adopted by many voices in the emerging "embodied cognition" school of thought, which argues that cognition is not exclusively brain-based, but a function of the interplay between the organism's body and its environment.

A central tenet of Gibson's is that our cognition and action are shaped by our environment (even if some of that environment is what we ourselves have made). As Louise Barrett says in her book *Beyond the Brain: How Body and Environment Shape Animal and Human Minds*,

> (w)hen we take a step back and consider how a cognitive process operates as a whole, we often find that the barrier between what's inside the skin and what's outside is often purely arbitrary, and, once we realize this, it dissolves (Barrett 2011a, p. 199).

That is, cognition (and therefore experience) is a property of the whole system, not just a reified, brain-originating abstraction. This point has been a key argument in what has been called the radical embodied cognition camp, which seeks not to just add embodiment onto mainstream cognitive science, but replace it altogether. As Barrett explains elsewhere,

> there's no such thing as disembodied cognition, really, if you're talking about living creatures. All of our cognition has to be embodied (…) (B)rains evolved in the service of action (Barrett 2011b).

Everything about our bodies, from the shape of our joints to the functions of our nervous and respiratory systems, and even our great big brains, evolved the way it did because of the structures in the environment around us. As Gibson eloquently states, "we were created by the world we live in" (Gibson 1979, p. 130).

Affordance An organizing principle behind all of Gibson's ideas on environmental perception is the concept of affordance, a principle Gibson himself invented. Affordances are the perceived properties of the environment that furnish opportunities for action.

The environment has a great deal of stuff going on in it—an "ambient sea of energy"—that is of little or no importance to the perceiver; what matters for perception most is what affords action in the environment for a particular organism (Gibson 1979, p. 57). That means affordances can be different for different perceivers, or even for the same perceiver in a different time with a different set of needs.

Writing in 1979, Gibson contends that his theory of affordances is "a radical departure from existing theories of value and meaning" (Gibson 1979, p. 140). Affordances are at the heart of all perception, and are intrinsic to how we experience and understand everything in the world. Perception is bound up entirely in what the environment means for bodily action. Can my body move through that space between the trees? Can I get across that river without drowning? Can I use that rock to crack open a coconut? At the core of our comprehension of the environment are these embodied considerations of what the environment affords for action.

In fact, perception only exists insofar as we perceive affordances. While at some more abstract, culturally-bound level, we might talk of color, time, location, space or motion, these are artificial frameworks. To see, taste, smell, feel or hear something is, quite literally, to see, taste, smell, feel or hear what that something affords (Gibson 1979, p. 240). Additionally, all affordances are essentially learned through action, through interacting with the environment. Anything we might think of as intuitive is actually something that is presenting enough previously learned affordances that it feels natural.

This original conception of affordance is not quite what most designers have encountered in their education. Typically, we hear talk of "adding an affordance" to something, but we have to consider the fact that it would not be a "something" unless it already had some sort of affording information to begin with. That is, understanding a particular affordance means understanding how it is nested within a broader context of other affording structures. We will look at what nesting means in a moment.

Invariance In order to have affordance, there has to be structure that is stable enough to be perceived, over time, as consistently affording physical activity. These are what Gibson calls invariant elements in the environment. For example, terrestrial creatures evolved in an environment with earth under our feet as quite literally the ground of all perception, and the core reason we have any structure in our environment at all. Gibson enumerates many invariant (as well as variant) elements of the environment, and how they form the structures we rely upon for orientation and action, from the way two solid surfaces intersect to create structure, to how the occluding edge of the human nose frames our vision.

These invariant properties are the base elements from which all structures we encounter emerge. These include, for example (Gibson 1979, p. 307):

- *Medium*, which is a substance that is insubstantial enough to permit locomotion, and which for terrestrial creatures is air;
- *Surfaces*, which are made of substances, that join together to create structures;
- *Objects*, which are surfaces that are topologically closed (for detached objects) or partially closed (for attached objects) in relation to surrounding surfaces;
- *Clutter*, which is the stuff in the environment that "occlude parts of the ground and divide the habitat into semi-enclosures" basically peripheral objects and surfaces that don't afford action in the moment, but affect what we perceive because it's "in the way".
- *Layout*, which refers to the "persisting arrangement of surfaces relative to one another and to the ground," where each different arrangement provides a particular set of affordances that differs from some other layout.
- *Event*, which is a change in the invariant structures of the environment, such as a change in layout, color or texture, or the existence of an environmental element. Events are at the core of how we perceive time. This explains, for example, why time feels like it is going faster or slower depending on our context.

This is only the barest summary of Gibson's environmental taxonomy, but it provides a framework from which we can extrapolate many useful concepts for how we create software-dependent environments. In fact, we already use some of these terms in similar ways in design practice.

In software environments, we depend on comprehension of *layout* as well as the affordances of *objects* as differentiated from mere underlying *surfaces*. We hear users talk of *clutter* but find that one user's clutter is another user's object. We see users trying to figure out what parts of a system they can move through (*medium*) versus parts that do not afford action. And especially as digital systems have more digital agency, we find users struggling to perceive and comprehend the *events* that occur in software environments, where cause-and-effect does not have to follow natural laws. These issues translate not only to the simulated-physical experience of interfaces, which draw objects like windows and mechanical controls onto the screen, but in semantic structures made only of words, and their relational structures found in lists, categorical hierarchies, and other organizational schemes.

8.5   The Principle of Nesting

Gibson explains that animals experience their environment as "nested", with subordinate and superordinate structures. As established above, "earth and sky" form the highest superordinate structure. At subordinate levels, there is more nesting:

"canyons are nested within mountains; trees are nested within canyons; leaves are nested within trees (...) there are forms within forms both up and down the scale of size (Gibson 1979, p. 9)". These are all, by the way, *invariants* in the environment. They establish the relatively persistent context within which we move, within which events occur, within which changes happen, both fast and slow. It is crucial to note that nesting is not the same as hierarchy. Gibson stresses that nesting

> would constitute a hierarchy except that this hierarchy is not categorical but full of transitions and overlaps. Hence, for the terrestrial environment, there is no special proper unit in terms of which it can be analyzed once and for all (Gibson 1979, p. 9).

By "categorical" Gibson means that the ecological environment is not structured in a single, logically absolute way; neither does it fit neatly into an abstracted set of categories. The ecological experience of an environment is more fluid, with "transitions and overlaps" rather than the mutually exclusive branching we see in an organizational chart or a hierarchical taxonomy.

Our perception of what is nested within what can shift based on our context or situational needs. As Gibson explains,

> (t)he theory of affordances rescues us from the philosophical muddle of assuming fixed classes of objects, each defined by its common features and then given a name (Gibson 1979, p. 134).

Perception itself does not fuss over categorical definition. When we find our way through our environment, our core cognitive activity is just working its way through structured surfaces, which can mean different things to us at different times. A stone is clutter one moment, but affords itself as a tool the next.

In information architecture practice, we see this principle at work when we use faceted taxonomies, which can accommodate multiple points of view: a scarf can be simultaneously a "knit" item, a "winter wear" item, and a general "accessory". This principle applies to places as well as objects: Twitter can be both a "status posting" medium and a "conversation platform", depending on how its affordances are being used. A corporate intranet could be mainly a "publication platform" for the Human Resources department, but mainly a "time entry portal" for a typical employee. Objects and places can both be multiple things at once to multiple perceivers, and they can even be different things over time to the same perceiver. Architectural schema work best when they accommodate these varying points of view.

8.6   Places

Places are a function of how an animal exists and subsists in the environment. "The habitat of an animal is made up of places" (Gibson 1979, p. 34). Gibson emphasizes these are not geometric points in a coordinate grid of space—an artificial construct. Ecologically, a place is defined by its affordances to a particular perceiver.

Places have a role in how we experience the environment as nested; and, like nesting, there are not necessarily sharp boundaries between places (Gibson 1979, p. 34). Gibson explains that "(a) very important kind of learning for animals and children is place-learning—learning the affordances of places and learning to distinguish among them—and way-finding, which culminate in the state of being oriented to the whole habitat and knowing where one is in the environment" (Gibson 1979, p. 240). If there is anything that has been a core concern of information architecture, it is finding one's way in an environment. It is easy to see, then, how understanding the way people perceive and comprehend physical places and the associations and paths between them is an important foundation for how people navigate digital-semantic environments.

8.7 The Ecological Foundation

I contend that physical (or ecological) information is the sort of information upon which all other sorts are based, and that Gibson's anatomy of the elements that make up the ecological environment (surface, object, event, etc.) can serve as a useful framework for how we think about and create all sorts of environments, including those we make or enhance with software.

But what does semantic structure, made with language, have to do with the sort of perception that allows not only humans but spiders and lizards to get around in the world? That brings us to the semantic mode.

8.8 Semantic Information

The semantic information mode is information from language for communication between people. Included in language are oral speech, gestures, writing, as well as graphical artifacts like photographs, icons, maps, and diagrams.

8.8.1 Semantic Affordance

So how is it that we can say language, which is traditionally thought of as abstract signification, has affordance, which we have established is all about physical structure and action? It is because language is not as abstract as we tend to think. In fact, it works by using similar cognitive and perceptual mechanisms that we use to act in the physical environment. From the first-person perspective of embodiment, *"there is no difference at all* between the two types of information" (Wilson and Golonka 2013).

Human communication puts new environmental structure into the world. For example, when I speak, I am vibrating the air, but what those vibrations *mean* has to be learned. When I write, I am encoding speech into physical markings on a surface, again adding to the environment, but decoding that writing into speech requires learning its semantic affordances as well. Gestures, pictures, and every semantic expression is creating some structural object or event among the surfaces of the environment. So, in this model, language is not information in and of itself. Rather, *language is environment*—structure we add to the natural and built environment, in order to convey some meaning. There is still affordance at work here, but of a different order. Language *conveys* information, but as environmental structure, not as information itself.

Gibson does not dwell on language in his work, but he does mention that "speech and language convey information of a certain sort from person to person" (Gibson 1979, p. 260). And he touches on a key difference between the sort of knowledge we acquire through physical information and that which we communicate through semantic information, pointing out that "(k)nowing by means of language makes knowing explicit instead of tacit. Language permits descriptions and pools the accumulated observations of our ancestors" and that language (including other semantic human-to-human communication artifacts like sculpture or painting) does not "permit firsthand experience (but) only experience at second hand" (Gibson 1979, p. 63).

Consider a lever on a slot machine. The intrinsically physical affordance information of the lever specifies that I can pull it down or push it up, but that's all. In order to know what it will do beyond its own movement, I have to either learn (through action and information pickup) or be told (through semantic information). In this way, the lever is behaving as a signifier, a symbol, that can stand for any number of things. Another lever might open a flood gate, while yet another might launch a missile. Like language, the lever depends on conventions, context and learning to be accurately meaningful.

Language behaves similarly. It presents many levers with many meanings that we have to learn over time. Saying the word "fire" affords merely the hearing of the vibrations (or its written form affords merely seeing marks on a surface). We have to look at its conventional context for an indication as to its most relevant import: "fire" can have to do with conflagration, pulling a trigger, losing a job, or a passionate emotion. The lever of "fire" has second-hand affordance that depends on human signification and convention, but it is still affordance. It's just an affordance that depends on the *convention* of learned meaning rather than the *laws* of ecological physics (Wilson and Golonka 2013).

8.8.2   Language as Infrastructure

In the words of embodiment theorist Andy Clark, language is "cognitive scaffolding" that we create as part of our shared environment (Clark 2008, p. 44). It is structure we add to the environment to create a sort of meta environment allowing us to accomplish more complex, collaborative, coordinated environmental activity. Clark points out that labels in particular are a sort of "augmented reality trick" we use to enhance our environment with human-made and human-taught affordances (Clark 2008, p. 46). That is, we augment our ability to work with the first-hand surfaces of the environment by introducing second-hand symbols for them.

This is the sort of information we most often mean when we talk about the information architecture practice of organizing and structuring information. But what is often missing is the realization that by creating and connecting labels through "mere" language we are actually creating environment. We are making places, not in a metaphorical sense, but in a literal sense of architecture as structures for human cohabitation.

This is especially true in software, where the scaffolding becomes the primary built environment or, in a sense, the map is used as territory. For example, a chat program is not a physically bounded place; it is a language construct that describes boundaries, within which people communicate with text. But, even in early versions of chat platforms, such as Internet Relay Chat (IRC), people converse with each other "as if in the same (real-life) room", sometimes to the point of living "parallel lives" online and off (Turkle 1995, p. 14).

Likewise, a hyperlink presents itself as just a label, but the hypertext protocol makes that label a portal into another place; the signifier affords embodied cognitive motion, which we intuitively experience as "going somewhere." If we gauge the reality of something by the degree it impacts human life, we would be hard pressed to say these online experiences are merely "virtual." They are places, made with language, that depend on the structural integrity of that language to be stable, coherent environments.

This stability can be affected by the structural integrity of linguistic meaning that is in the broader environmental context. Anyone who has significant experience working across the layers of an organization's information stack from the bowels of IT data architectures to the menu structure of a mobile app can attest to the chaos and confusion that results from semantic fragmentation. If the marketing department decides to call a product line by a name that the rest of the infrastructure does not recognize, suddenly customers cannot find what they need, and customer service representatives have to painfully translate for irate shoppers. From org charts to document metadata, labels matter for organizational effectiveness as much as any office building blueprint or cubicle layout.

8.8.3   Loops of Least Resistance

Even though semantic information is more central and concrete to human cognitive experience than we may realize, there are still important differences in how we perceive semantic versus ecological affordance. For one thing, semantic information takes more work than physical information, and our bodies tend to use whatever route is easiest for figuring out our surroundings. Cognition uses many loops between the perceiver and the environment, making use of information intrinsic to the environment or in the structures of the body, or in language, but it tends to use the loops that require the least effort. According to Clark, this is partly described by something called the Principle of Ecological Assembly, or "PEA." The "cognizer tends to recruit, on the spot, whatever mix of problem-solving resources will yield an acceptable result with minimal effort." (Clark 2008, p. 13)

That is, our cognition "satisfices" to use the term coined by economist and social scientist Herbert A. Simon, who argued (in a train of thought similar to Gibson's) that we do not optimize our decisions and actions in a purely logical way, but with "bounded rationality" that is constrained by our cognitive limitations.

Teasing apart the way human perception picks up affordance from semantic versus physical information is a key area for understanding how people comprehend the simulated physicality of software interfaces. For example, when we see users close pop-up windows without fully reading them, we are seeing an organism clearing clutter out of the way in order to keep moving even if the window was an important alert about the environment underneath it. This analysis is also important for how people make their way through textual semantic structures, tapping or clicking links that satisfice for perception/action toward meeting some need.

8.8.4   *Navigating is Understanding*

The distinction between physical and semantic information is also key for understanding how people navigate among labels and connections, and how they perceive the invariant or variant elements of a semantically dependent environment.

In a giant storage facility, where all the doors and hallways look the same, labels might be the only useful differentiating invariant structure available for wayfinding. Likewise, in a news website, where the actual content might change and shift over time, the labels that establish the persistent structures available functional place-making—labels like "Your Account" or "Home" as well as stable category labels for the site's content—are often the only invariant structures a user can count on for orientation in that environment.

Connecting language to physically embodied cognition in this way also informs how we understand concepts like "information foraging" and "information scent". We "satisfice". We do not logically figure out the most efficient path to something, but we sniff our way to what feels relevant, through "passive, undirected behavior". (Bates 2002). We work our way through semantic information environments much as we do through the physical world.

Extend these issues to the omni-contextual scenarios of personal health monitoring devices, smart homes, and self-driving cars, and we can see how such fluid complexity—much of it hidden from everyday perception—requires even more stable, invariant structures of language to make sense of it all.

Navigation of information environments is not merely a supplementary activity relegated to navigation objects such as software menus, any more than we navigate a city by looking only at a map. We utilize as much of the environment as will have us. Navigation is something humans have been doing since before they were human. It is part of the perception-action loop described by Gibson, where we move in an environment in order to comprehend it so that we can keep moving. As Resmini and Rosati put it in *Pervasive Information Architecture*, "(w)e say navigate but really mean understand" (Resmini and Rosati 2011, p. 66). For a species that lives as much in language as it does in physical places, the structures of semantic environments matter a great deal not only for discrete tasks, but for human existence in general.

Our natural state is to understand our world by probing and sensing the whole environment, not just the artificial navigation bits. An embodied perspective takes us out of the mechanistic paradigm of information storage-and-retrieval, and brings us to a broader, richer understanding of semantic information as an essential part of our human habitat. Understanding how language affords action, and how it structures and sometimes wholly comprises environments, is central to how we mold and shape the materials of information architecture.

8.9 Digital Information

Before the rise of ubiquitous digital networks, we did not have to think so hard about all this. People spent the majority of their lives only needing to understand physical places, with supplementary semantic objects, such as road signs or newspapers. Digital networks and particularly the hyperlink allowed semantic information to become something we can make explicitly inhabited places out of in a way that we could not before. It caused a conflation of object and place, and complicated what we mean when we say "here" and "there".

This disruption of context is in part because the digital information mode is not made for human consumption. It is information as code for machines, used in the black box realm of computers transmitting and receiving between one another. In other words, it is the Claude Shannon framing of information: coded symbols and rules (1949), made for (and even by) computing devices, in a way that makes it ideal for those devices by stripping human context out of the mix. According to Shannon, the "semantic aspects of communication are irrelevant to (solving) the engineering problem" of transmission and reception. This sort of information has affordance, but for artificial creatures of pure logic, not flesh-and-bone organisms.

8.9.1 Digital Influence

Humans do not comprehend the digital information mode in its native state, but we experience its effects, both systematically and culturally. For example, when we see confusing error codes, or encounter digital-system structures that make sense to the machine but not to the user, we are experiencing some of the negative effects of digital information. These outputs have been translated to have a bit of semantic affordance for something or someone, but not for regular people during everyday activity. More disconcerting problems can happen when digital systems have agency, and can make decisions for us without communicating them to us at all. This can confound our perception's innate expectations, since we evolved in an environment where the cause-and-effect of an *object's* affordance and a resulting *event* was typically observable and tangible. Software environments have no natural physical laws they have to follow, which exacerbates this de-contextualizing of mechanical causation. When a social platform like Facebook automatically adds us to a public list or news feed because we took some action elsewhere, not realizing these contexts were connected, it can have devastating consequences.

Of course, there are positive effects, such as the ability to have digital networks and devices in the first place. These are wondrous, beneficial technologies when architected responsibly. But doing so can be terribly challenging. There are often cultural assumptions that arise from the priority we place on the digital framing of information, such as preferring pure hierarchy, workflow efficiency and structural linearity over the more organic, messy, and fluidly nested way in which people actually perceive and comprehend their environments. When we assume that people will comprehend their environment with the same comprehensive, logical perception as a screen-scraping search bot, we lose sight of what makes such an environment good for human life.

8.9.2   Where We Live

We do not live in the digital dimension, we live in the physical-and-semantic dimension. A major task of information architecture is to push the things made and enhanced with digital information further toward being comprehensible, habitable, and ecologically sound environments for human beings.

One way in which information architecture accomplishes this task is by creating bridges between two different sorts of ontology. One sort of ontology (in its original meaning) is the very human question of the nature of being. The other sort is from information science, where it means a formal representation of concepts in a given domain, so that a computer has a useful understanding of those concepts.

While most users of digital systems are not explicitly pondering the philosophical question of existence, they most definitely are attempting to comprehend and act within their environment from a tacit set of ontological assumptions about the nature of the places and actions afforded there. Much of information architecture practice is focused on discovering what those embodied ontological assumptions are. Our most-used methods and tools, such as mental models, card sorting, or user journeys, are largely about figuring out this bridge between what computers can know and what people understand.

As digital networks allow us to carry more and more of our shared reality across many disparate places and situations, information architecture is becoming even more essential for establishing and cultivating, as Jorge Arango frames it, "the structural integrity of meaning across contexts" (Arango 2013). Digital information does not do this work on its own any more than raw minerals self-organize into skyscrapers. It takes architectural work to establish the structures needed for our ecologically and semantically driven cognition, not just for finding, but for dwelling.

8.10   The New Human Environment

At the 1976 American Institute of Architects gathering in Philadelphia, organizer Richard Saul Wurman made a case that practitioners not only be architects but *information* architects. Since the rise of the Internet, the need has become only greater. Pervasive technologies have gone well past the point of making us feel as if we are (as the expression goes) "drinking from a fire-hose." Information has changed the hose, the hydrant, the firehouse, and the city itself.

We now have a new kind of environment that we have created for ourselves—one that is fundamentally different from the environments of the generations before us. We are still learning the nature of the new world we have made. And yet, we are still basically the same animals we were before the Internet, or electricity, or even the invention of writing.

As Peter Morville states in his groundbreaking *Ambient Findability*, "(t)he proving grounds have shifted from natural and built environments to the noosphere, a world defined by symbols and semantics" (Morville 2005, p. 41). If there is a "re-framing" for information architecture, it is partly in seeing more clearly the problems we were solving all along: figuring out how language forms environments in more explicit, concrete ways than ever before. There is much work to be done to make this new environment one in which our bodies can dwell as naturally as our minds.

References

AIFIA.org. (2002). The Asilomar Institute for Information Architecture (now the Information Architecture Institute). http://web.archive.org/web/20021031211246/http://www.aifia.org/pg/about_aifia.php. Accessed Jan 2014.

Arango, J. (2013). For the World Wide Web. http://www.jarango.com/blog/2013/06/28/for-the-world-wide-web/. Accessed Jan 2014.

Barrett, L. (2011a). *Beyond the brain: How body and environment shape animal and human minds*. Princeton: Princeton University Press.

Barrett, L. (2011b). Embodiment: Taking sociality seriously. Video. University of Oxford Podcasts. http://podcasts.ox.ac.uk/embodiment-taking-sociality-seriously. Accessed Jan 2014.

Bates, M. (2002). *Toward an integrated model of information seeking and searching*. Fourth international conference on information needs, seeking and use in different contexts, New review of information behaviour research, Issue 3, pp. 1–15.

Champeon, S. (1997). Lou Rosenfeld, web architect. A jaundiced eye. http://a.jaundicedeye.com/stuck/archive/050897/article.html. Accessed Jan 2014.

Clark, A. (2008). *Supersizing the mind: Embodiment, action, and cognitive extension*. New York: Oxford University Press.

Dang, H. D., & Allen, P. K. (2012). *Semantic grasping: Planning robotic grasps functionally suitable for an object manipulation task*. IEEE/RSJ International conference on intelligent robots and systems.

Evans, V. (2006). Lexical concepts, cognitive models and meaning-construction. *Cognitive Linguistics, 17*(4), 491–534.

Garrett, J. J. (2009) The memphis plenary. http://www.jjg.net/ia/memphis/. Accessed Dec 2013.

Gibson, J. J. (1979). *The ecological approach to visual perception*. Boston: Houghton Mifflin.

Hinton, A. (2002). 25 theses. http://iainstitute.org/en/learn/research/25_theses.php. Accessed Jan 2014.

Hobbs, J., Fenn, T., & Resmini, A. (2010). Maturing a practice. *Journal of Information Architecture, 2*(1), 37–54. (http://journalofia.org/volume2/issue1/04-hobbs//).

Morville, P. (2005). *Ambient findability*. Sebastopol: O'Reilly Media.

Resmini, A., & Rosati, L. (2011). *Pervasive information architecture: Designing cross-channel user experiences*. Burlington: Morgan Kaufmann.

Shannon, C. E. (1949). *A mathematical theory of communication*. Urbana: University of Illinois Press. (Reprinted with corrections from *The Bell System Technical Journal, 27,* 379–423, 623–656).

Turkle, S. (1995). *Life on the screen: Identity in the age of the internet*. New York: Simon & Schuster.

Wilson, A. (2011). Chemero (2009) Chapter 9—The metaphysics of radical embodiment. Notes from two scientific psychologists. http://psychsciencenotes.blogspot.com/2011/06/chemero-2009-chapter-9-metaphysics-of.html. Accessed Jan 2014.

Wilson, A. D., & Golonka, S. (2013). Embodied cognition is not what you think it is. *Frontiers in Psychology, 4,* 58. doi:10.3389/fpsyg.2013.00058.

Young, G. (2006). Are different affordances subserved by different neural pathways? *Brain and Cognition, 62*(2), 134–142. (http://dx.doi.org/10.1016/j.bandc.2006.04.002).

Chapter 9
Dutch Uncles, Ducks and Decorated Sheds— Notes on the Intertwingularity of Meaning and Structure in Information Architecture

Dan Klyn

Abstract On what basis can and ought one assess the relative merits of a given work of information architecture? In 2009, Jesse James Garrett pointed to the non-existence of such a normative theory and the community of practice's consequent inability to indicate "what good means" as evidence that information architecture is not a proper discipline. Garrett's rallying cry was for a wholesale reframing of that community in terms of User Experience Design, with human engagement as its center. In this chapter, I draw from the work of architects Denise Scott Brown and Robert Venturi to counter-propose a co-occurring reframing of the mostly-digital sense- and place-making work of information architecture in the normative terms of architecture, where the appropriate interplay of meaning and structural form comprises the basis of what good means.

9.1 Dutch Uncles

Convenience stores and service stations where I live have recently introduced a change in the choreography of how one is meant to interact with the gas pumps. The new procedure requires keying-in one's 5-digit postal code as a pre-step to paying at the pump with a credit card.

I'm sure this additional step in what had previously been a more streamlined process has been proven (with math!) to be worth the implementation effort for the businesses who are taking the payments. But I doubt the designers and accountants behind these machinations have the data to explain the marked increase in delight I now experience in the prelude to paying for and then refilling my car's fuel tank.

4-9-4-2-6: the first number I ever memorized on purpose.

This weekly opportunity to reply to the blinking cursor on the gas pump's LCD display with the earliest of cognitive muscle memories fills me with toddler glee: for a moment I'm 4 years old again and a very good boy reciting my ZIP code when prompted for it.

D. Klyn (✉)
University of Michigan, Ann Arbor, USA
e-mail: dan@understandinggroup.com

A. Resmini (ed.), *Reframing Information Architecture,* Human-Computer Interaction Series,   119
DOI 10.1007/978-3-319-06492-5_9, © Springer International Publishing Switzerland 2014

Today, as an adult, I once again reside in the place I grew up. Ten miles west is an "x" that marks the spot of the surrounding culture's literal wellspring and figurative ground zero—a city that's five or six times bigger than and marked with a code just a few digits off from mine: Holland.

Like the nearby villages and burghs within its cultural blast radius (e.g. Overisel, Drenthe, Vriesland, Zeeland), Holland got its name from the Dutch Calvinists who were compelled to emigrate here in the 1840s under the legendarily severe leadership of a preacher/entrepreneur by the name of Albertus van Raalte.

Each spring, thousands of visitors come to Holland to admire the tulips and attend daily parades where locals march themselves and their kids down the main street in old-timey Dutch costumes. Postcards and buttons spinning in wire-racked orbit on the countertops of the shops are a blur of windmills and flowers and *klompen* dancers, all of it begging the question: wooden shoe rather be Dutch?

Having been born-and-raised and now once again residing in such a place—a place where bumper stickers read "If You Ain't Dutch, You Ain't Much"—I was surprised recently to see a South African architect describe her professional role as being that of a "Dutch uncle" to younger colleagues in contemporary practice.

Dutch uncle? It was an appellation I'd never heard before. When all of one's uncles are Dutch, one never hears of a Dutch uncle.

After a quick bit of Googling to see what this architect might have meant, I found the explanation to ring true. Both in terms of the signifier as well as with regard to the signified. Dutch uncle: a person giving firm but benevolent advice.

The architect dispensing this firm-yet-benevolent advice is a personal hero: the inimitable Denise Scott Brown. Part of the purpose of the present essay is to posit Scott Brown's point of view and that of her partner Robert Venturi on the interplay of meaning and structure in architecture as quite relevant (if not essential) to contemporary information architecture practice. But first, before I make the case for information architects as Netherlandic nieces and nephews of Venturi and Scott Brown I need to spend a few words about the Dutch uncles we have already got.

9.2   The Memphis Plenary

March 22 2009, Memphis, Tennessee. Jesse James Garrett delivers the closing plenary address at the 10th-annual Information Architecture Summit. If ever there were an act of Dutch uncle-ing in the IA community, this is it, although one's ability to see the benevolence in Garrett's rhetorical tour de force is perhaps mutually occluded by the attention that has been paid to that part of the speech where he says "there's no such thing as information architects."

In the softer glow of hindsight, I read Mr. Garrett's declaration as a suspended sentence, not a summary judgment; as a purposeful piece of provocation—a preemptive move against the threat of stagnation in the inadequately-defined would-be discipline of information architecture. When viewed from the interpretive lens of the Dutch uncle, Garrett's grilling in Memphis can be understood as a sort of heuristic checklist for determining the future conditions within which one could credibly say that there *are* such things as information architects:

> Do you know good IA when you see it? And can different people have different ideas about the qualities of a good solution or a bad one, based on their philosophical approach to their work?
> Will there ever be a controversial work of information architecture? Something we argue about the merits of? A work that has admirers and detractors alike?
> We don't have a language of critique. Until we have ways to describe the qualities of an information architecture, we won't be able to tell good IA from bad IA. All we'll ever be able to do is judge processes.

The existence of a language of critique presupposes the existence of an underlying—and from Garrett's point of view in 2009, non-existent—theory for differentiating good from bad information architecture.[1] And how does one establish a normative theory of information architecture in the absence of a straightforward definition of information architecture? As Resmini and Rosati (2011) noted,

> The debate on what information architecture is and how it should be defined properly is almost 20 years old and is beginning to rival the one still enveloping "information science" and dating back to the mid-1950s.

I was there, in the ballroom at the Peabody Hotel in Memphis, when Mr. Garrett read out his suspended death sentence for information architecture, and my diverging point of view on the "missing" definition, normative theory, and language of critique for information architecture is that these pretexts to legitimacy (or to extend the judge-jury-and-executioner analogy, clemency) were not so much missing in 2009 as they were unevenly distributed.

As Mr. Garrett noted elsewhere in his Memphis plenary, the distinction between information architecture and interaction design lacked meaningful difference in 2009, and was being played out in the marketplace as a zero-sum game. Garrett's counter-proposal to mutually assured destruction: move the proverbial goalposts and fundamentally change the game:

> There are no information architects. There are no interaction designers. There are only, and only ever have been, user experience designers.

9.3   Bounded and Centered Sets

My preferred approach to explaining the particular genius of Mr. Garrett's Peabody polemic borrows from the teachings of a Quaker theologian named John Wimber, who in turn borrowed from the teachings of a branch of mathematics called *set theory* to model the dynamics of intentional communities.

---

[1] Andrea Resmini explored Garrett's closing plenary in his own closing plenary at the ASIS&T European Information Architecture Summit in 2013, explicitly connecting the need of a language of critique to the evolution of a poetics of information architecture (Resmini 2013a).

In Wimber's formulation, an intentional community like that of the Dutch Calvinists of Holland, Michigan, is a *bounded set*. Membership in bounded sets is contingent upon acceptance of and demonstrated compliance with particular rules. Calvinism's definitional boundary has been sacrosanct for more than a hundred years, and reified in the Dutch-descended-yet-English-speaking community by way of a particularly relevant acronym: TULIP.[2]

Weighing-in on one of the information architecture community's seemingly-endless definitional boundary-battles on the Information Architecture Institute's email list in September of 2010, institute founder and bona fide Dutch Uncle Christina Wodtke replied to a stereotypically fractious thread with a characteristically incisive Youtube link[3] of a Monty Python clip from Life of Brian in which the rag-tag members of Judean People's Front rail against the People's Front of Judea for being "splitters".

The clip illustrated the problem eloquently. Bounded sets become dysfunctional in proportion to the ambiguity of their boundaries. Hilarity is always just a phoneme or fat-fingered acronym away.

In 2009, with interaction designers, information architects and user experience designers attending the same events, going after the same jobs and offering identically-named deliverables in their respective scopes-of-work, what Garrett proposed was not a repair job on the convoluted boundaries that had previously circumscribed these communities of practice. As I re-read and recollect that speech I do not see Garrett making an argument for conflating information architecture and interaction design within a rehabilitated bounded set called user experience design. What I see and hear him doing there is a wholesale reframing of the underlying set theory—positing an alternate structure for organizing the people in that ballroom and for explaining what that group is about along the lines of what Wimber would call a *centered set*. Wimber's teachings eventually became the basis for a movement within Christianity known as The Vineyard, and one of their congregations in Southeast Michigan explains centered sets especially well[4]:

> The centered set approach is like gathering cats rather than herding cattle. The center is the pail of milk that draws the cats.

With centered sets, there is no definitional boundary. And what's more, an individual's proximity to the center of the set does not matter all that much. What matters with a centered set is direction. Any cat that is pointed in the direction of the pail is considered to be a member of the set.

This is precisely what Mr. Garrett proposed in Memphis—that the people, processes and methodologies represented in that ballroom were all more-or-less pointing at the same thing. Mr. Garrett insists that what we do is not ultimately centered on users, information, architecture, interaction or design.

---

[2] http://calvinistcorner.com/tulip.htm.

[3] http://www.youtube.com/watch?v=gb_qHP7VaZE.

[4] Ann Arbor Vineyard Church (2014) http://annarborvineyard.org/about/what-we-believe/a-centered-set-church.

> Engagement is what it's all about. Our work exists to be engaged with. In some sense, if no
> one engages with our work it doesn't exist (Garrett 2009).

In other words, the milk in the pail at the center of the gathering of user experience cats is human engagement.

I think the articulation of this argument was and is brilliant for a number of reasons, and that regardless of Mr. Garrett's intentions for what would follow his rhetorical *coup de grace*, recasting user experience as a practically boundless galaxy with engagement at its center had the benevolent effect of pre-empting further internecine escalations and mutual exclusions in the wider universe of markets and ideas. From Memphis forward, it was easier to just call all of this user experience and not cause a fuss. But if user experience is recast as an engagement-centric galaxy then, perhaps inadvertently, it also begs the question of what *else* is in the universe.

April 6 2013, Baltimore, USA. At the fourteenth ASIS&T IA Summit, as part of a presentation titled "Links, Nodes and Order" (Arango 2013), Jorge Arango delivers a tacit rejection of bounded-set framing for information architecture in the course of proposing information architecture as the only community of practice with the structural integrity of meaning as its unique concern and gravitational center (Fig. 9.1).

Information architecture as a community of practice with the structural integrity of meaning at its center provides (at last) a highly serviceable base upon which normative theories for information architecture may begin to build themselves. And reframing information architecture as its own distinct galaxy with structure and meaning at the center paves the desire lines that Wodtke, Resmini, Hinton, and Arango (among others) have long been tracing into information architecture from architecture.

Moreover, adjacent galaxies can and do overlap: focus on one of them does not necessarily occlude visibility into or even presence within the other. In the physical universe they form what astronomers call an occulting pair—two systems aligned in ways that neither preclude nor require gravitational interaction.

9.4   Learning From Vitruvius and Las Vegas

Because architecture in the built environment is *all about* the interplay of structure and meaning, and given the reframing around structure and meaning (Arango et al. 2011; Resmini 2013b), information architecture is correctly seen as situated within the jurisdiction of normative theories of what makes "good" and "bad" architecture. Or at least: within the jurisdiction of those theories of architecture explicitly set up in terms of structure and meaning.

The question of how one ought to design structure with respect to meaning provides a through-line from "the discipline's most venerable theoretical foundation" in the writings of the Roman architect Vitruvius (Costanzo 2012) in the first-century C.E. to the work of some but not all architects in contemporary practice.

Fig. 9.1 Information
architecture cats around
meaning-bucket. Illustration
by E. Marcks. Copyright
2013 The Understanding
Group, used under
permission

Yale University Howard H. Newman Professor Karsten Harries connects the
philosophical dots across millennia from Vitruvius to our aforementioned Dutch
Uncles Robert Venturi and Denise Scott Brown while noting that their shared sym-
pathies begin with recognition of the basic function of architecture as that

> of interpreting the world as a meaningful order in which the individual can find his place in
> the midst of nature and in the midst of a community.

In the autumn of 1968 Scott Brown, Venturi and Steven Izenour undertook a now-
legendary examination of the interplay of meaning and architectural form in a research project at the Yale School of Art and Architecture entitled "Learning from
Las Vegas". Part of the stated purpose of the project was "evolving the traditional
architectural 'studio' into a new tool for teaching architecture and finding graphic
means, more suitable than those used now by architects and planners, to describe
'urban sprawl' urbanism and particularly the commercial strip" (Venturi et al. 1972).

The work of the studio and the results of its research were published in book
form by MIT Press in 1972, and "Learning from Las Vegas" went on in multiple
re-printings to provide the theoretical foundation for much of what would soon be
labeled postmodernism. The studio's quest for more suitable means for describing

Fig. 9.2 The Duck and its "more modest companion" the Decorated Shed. (Venturi et al. 1972, p. 65)

the operative conditions that architects and planners confronted in contemporary culture resulted in a number of innovations in information visualization and visual analysis—many of which were elided, down- or up- scaled into illegibility or entirely absent in the second and subsequent printings.

What remains vivid, though, across all editions and printings—both in depiction as well as in rhetoric—is its framework of "Ducks" and "Decorated Sheds" as a normative theory for governing the congress of meaning and structure in architecture. As I have come to know them, I suspect that the teachings encoded in the various printings of *Learning From Las Vegas* and those of Vitruvius as rendered in his *Ten Books on Architecture* are prosaic, polemic and portentous enough to act as rhetorical centrifuge for enriching a critical mass of normative theory for information architecture.

And while the rationale I've built thus far wants to spin off into a wholesale cross-appropriation of twenty centuries of architecture theory to the practice of information architecture, I'll show how the fissile duality of Ducks and Decorated Sheds lends itself especially well to weaponization with the Vitruvian triad of "firmness, commodity, and delight" in the specific context of structures and places made of information.

9.5   Ducks and Decorated Sheds

The dialectic of Ducks and Sheds proceeds from Scott Brown and Venturi's shared "witty and possibly reckless cultural pessimism" (Vinegar 2008), and might at first seem incongruous when compared to the imperial optimism and systematic sincerity in the *Ten Books on Architecture*. Nevertheless and with an uncharacteristic absence of irony, Venturi traces the conditions in architecture that the Ducks-and-Sheds model is meant to mediate directly back to Vitruvius (Fig. 9.2):

> Architecture is necessarily complex and contradictory in its very inclusion of the traditional Vitruvian elements (Venturi 1965).

The centrality of Vitruvian ethics to Venturi's work appears to have been amplified as his thinking, practice and personal life became conjoined with those of Scott Brown in the late 1960s. Together with Izenour in *LLV* they level a broad critique of the architectural "Ducks" resulting from Bauhaus and International Style

Fig. 9.3 Vitruvius vs
Gropius in Venturi and Scott
Brown's approach. Adapted
from Costanzo 2012

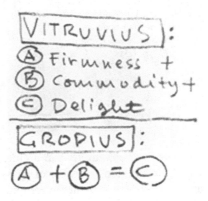

approaches to architecture, and call Walter Gropius up to the blackboard for a lesson
in balancing the Vitruvian equation (Fig. 9.3).

Gropius promised to heal the rift between beauty and reason" (Harries 1983), but
for the authors of "Learning from Las Vegas" the reductive math of high Modernism does not actually add up. They commiserate with the modernist desire to design
architecture as a totality, but point to (while painting it) the contrast between the
"dead ducks" of pure clean Modernism and the "messy vitality" of the decorated
sheds along the Las Vegas strip as the poles of a duality for sussing out a postmodern normative theory for architecture.

Because it restricts the range of what is permissible with architectural form to
only those modalities derived from working out the sum of firmness plus utility,
Venturi, Scott Brown and Izenour argue that Modernism can only hatch Ducks.

A Duck is a building whose architectural systems of space, structure, and program are submerged and distorted by an overall symbolic form; in other words, a
building-becoming-sculpture. In contrast, the Decorated Shed is a building whose
systems of space and structure are directly at the service of program, and ornament
is applied independently of them.

> The Decorated Shed was intended as a return to the more complete understanding of archi-
> tectural function encapsulated in the Vitruvian triad (Costanzo 2012).

To grossly oversimplify, the immediate lesson of "Learning From Las Vegas" for
architects and planners in the built environment is: don't Duck.

A duck-shaped building that sells duck eggs is presented as emblematic of Modernist ideals regarding the interplay of order, meaning and structure in architecture
that are based on the dichotomy of either/or. Architects make selections from a
bounded set of formal considerations, and the boundary for what is in and out of
consideration is clean. Heroic, even: *form (ever) follows function.*

Venturi, Scott Brown and Izenour's Decorated Shed resists being read as an em-
blem of anything, supplying and relying upon external signage and applied surface
graphics to close the gap between the "boring" and "ordinary" nature of a shed and
what is meant by and for the realization of the project.

What is understood regarding the nature of order, meaning and structure in the work of Venturi and Scott Brown is non dual, parrying the Modernist's either/or with a Vitruvian *yet*. Or as Scott Brown has said variously: *form follows forces*.

From this postmodern viewpoint, architects make selections from a more loosely regulated set of formal considerations where complexity and contradiction are to be expected—even embraced:

> When Robert Venturi writes of 'contradiction' in architecture, he is not supposing that a building can actually assert a self-contradictory sentence, but is speaking of exemplification by a building of forms that give rise when juxtaposed to expectations that contravene each other (Goodman 1985).

Elsewhere in the book the authors pair the analogy of gloves and mittens with that of Ducks and Decorated Sheds in enumerating the relative virtues of a loose coupling between structural form and functional requirements:

> The forms of building do not fit, like a glove on a hand, over the complex, unpredictable and sometimes intangible elements of realistic programs.

The reason Ducks are usually less good than Decorated Sheds is because, as Venturi says, "more is not less" (Venturi 1965). The plenitude of unpredictable and intangible requirements that project owners and end-users will realistically express, and the overlapping contexts those needs are smeared across means that one reliable way to differentiate good and less good approaches to architecture is in terms of how much or little complexity and contradiction they afford.

In other words: when the "fingers" of the program to be accommodated in the act of building promise to wiggle around and change in number and in orientation relative to each other on an ongoing basis, what is good is to build mittens not gloves. Sheds, not Ducks. Architectures with as little articulation of the under-girding structures as possible.

And in situations where the affect of what is meant by and through the realization of the project is flattened by the ordinariness of un-articulated shed-like structural forms, Venturi and Scott Brown propose animating and amplifying these meanings through the application of graphics, iconography and symbols to the surfaces of what is being built. This way, when what is meant and understood by the built project changes, the tactics and materials arrayed most closely to that meaning are easily and inexpensively updated.

9.6 Very Good Is Less than Good

In his 1966 introduction to the first edition of *Complexity and Contradiction in Architecture*, Vincent Scully waxes disapproving of the then-contemporary assessment of Venturi's work:

> It is no wonder Venturi's buildings have not found ready acceptance; they have been both too new and, for all their "accommodation" of complexity, too truly simple and unassuming for this affluent decade.

Venturi and Scott Brown's architecture is, in their own words, "second glance architecture." "Boring," even. Architecture where all three members of the Vitruvian triad are accounted for and appropriately balanced with regard to the project's situatedness along a continuum between the Duck and the Decorated Shed. What is good architecture like? As far as Denise Scott Brown is concerned:

> Accommodating rather than constricting. Revelatory rather than reductive (Venturi and Scott Brown 2004).

What are good buildings like then? She continues:

> Accommodate multiple options over generations rather than meet functional mandates for the first generation only; Face hard problems, rather than ignore them to fit into a desired form; Enter into a discernable and ongoing discussion with context; Allow many interpretations rather than one truth; Reveal rather than demonstrate.

This to me is a sensibility for what good means in architecture that is aligned quite closely with and in deep ethical agreement with what Louis Kahn meant when he said "very good is less than good" (Wurman 1986).

With regard to the intertwingularity of meaning and structural form in information architecture, what does good mean? The same thing it means in regular-old architecture.

References

Ann Arbor Vineyard Church. (2014). A centered set church. http://annarborvineyard.org/about/what-we-believe/a-centered-set-church. Accessed Jan 2014.

Arango, J. (2013). Links, nodes, and order—A unified theory of information architecture. http://www.jarango.com/blog/2013/04/07/links-nodes-order/. Accessed Jan 2014.

Arango, J., Hinton, A., and Resmini, A. (2011). More than a metaphor. Proceedings of the 12th ASIS&T IA Summit.

Costanzo, D. R. (2012). Venturi and Scott Brown as functionalists: Venustas and the Decorated Shed. *Cloud-Cuckoo-Land, 32,* 10–25.

Garrett, J. J. (2009). The Memphis Plenary. http://jjg.net/ia/memphis. Accessed Dec 2013.

Goodman, N. (1985). How buildings mean. *Critical Inquiry, 11*(4), 642–653.

Harries, K. (1983). Thoughts on a non-arbitrary architecture. *Perspecta, 20,* 9–20.

Marks, E. (2013). https://www.twitter.com/mectoamore. Accessed Dec 2013.

Resmini, A. (2012). What is Cross-channel?. http://andrearesmini.com/blog/what-is-crosschannel. Accessed Dec 2013.

Resmini, A. (2013a). The poetics of information architecture. Closing plenary. ASIS&T European Information Architecture Summit 2013. http://www.slideshare.net/resmini/the-poetics-of-information-architecture-26991604. Accessed Jan 2014.

Resmini, A. (2013b). Les architectures d'information. Etudes de Communication (Online). Vol. 41. http://edc.revues.org/5380. Accessed Jan 2014.

Resmini, A., & Rosati, L. (2011). *Pervasive information architecture—designing cross-channel user experiences*. San Mateo: Morgan Kaufmann.

Rodell, S. (2008). *The influence of Robert Venturi on Louis Kahn*. Masters Thesis, School of Architecture of Washington State University.

Venturi, R. (1965). Complexity and contradiction in architecture: Selections from a forthcoming book. *Perspecta, 9*(10), 17–56.

Venturi, R., & Scott Brown, D. (2004). *Architecture as signs and systems for a mannerist time.* Cambridge: Harvard University Press.

Venturi, R., Scott Brown, D., & Izenour, S. (1972). *Learning from Las Vegas.* Cambridge: MIT Press.

Vinegar, A. (2008). *I am a monument-on learning from Las Vegas.* Cambridge: MIT Press.

Vinegar, A., & Golec, M. J. (2009). *Relearning from Las Vegas.* Minneapolis:University of Minnesota Press.

Wurman, R. S. (1986). *What will be has always been: The words of Louis I. Kahn.* New York: Rizzoli Access Press.

Chapter 10
Representing Information Across Channels

David Peter Simon

Abstract Substantial progress has been made in using information architecture for different mediums and across different channels. NPR's COPE System—Create Once, Publish Everywhere—is just one example of creating flexible content for cross-channel ecosystems, spanning data entry to presentation layer. In this position piece, I reflect on the relationship between content presentation and evolving hardware. I posit that information architecture is a key practice in rendering device agnostic content, exploring the ways in which the structural design of information helps to bring into being a near seamless experience for users mentally navigating different environments. I use three specific case studies from three different organizations—Amazon, NPR, and Facebook—so as to illustrate how the structuring of data was a critical aspect in representing information across channels.

10.1 Pure Information Representation Versus Structured Presentation

The idea of presenting information in flexible form for different devices goes back to at least the very initial days of developing graphical user interfaces (GUI). For instance, early Web designers targeted a variety of screen resolutions, dealing with browsers that would consume information differently, such as dissimilar color palettes. One example of this was dithering: a technique used to fabricate color depth in images.

According to Pins and Hild (2013), dithering allowed for "a way to produce an image on hardware that would otherwise be incapable of displaying it". While not the best practice for preserving the integrity of information, it allowed for colors that could not be found, due to device constraints, to reproduce content at seemingly similar quality. The figure below illustrates dithering an image in practice (Fig. 10.1).

More recently, Responsive Web Design (RWD) has gained visibility and traction among the software development community, specifically among user interface

D. P. Simon (✉)
ThoughtWorks, London, UK
e-mail: dps@thoughtworks.com

A. Resmini (ed.), *Reframing Information Architecture,* Human-Computer Interaction Series,   131
DOI 10.1007/978-3-319-06492-5_10, © Springer International Publishing Switzerland 2014

Fig. 10.1 Dithering. (Source: Wikipedia)

(UI) developers who have the intent of presenting information in a universal form. Ethan Marcotte, the designer who coined the term RWD and first explored its opportunities, explained how, "Now, more than ever, we're designing work meant to be viewed along a gradient of different experiences" (Marcotte 2010).

However, the industry's subsequent dwelling on the adaptiveness of presentation has begun to confuse the foreground with an invisible background, skipping over "old fashion" questions about structuring and organizing information. Techniques like media queries, which are a much-discussed CSS3 extension that grants user interface developers control on how content should adapt to conditions such as screen resolution Roberts (2014), are only one specimen of new opportunities for representing information across channels.

Instead of preoccupying ourselves with UI development techniques, businesses ought to focus on how to produce ecosystems, without limiting themselves to representational implementation. RWD is a fantastic technique for the industry to discuss, but it's a technique—simply that. As Andrew Hinton once questioned, "Is it stating the obvious to say responsive web design is a valuable technique, but it's not a strategy?" (Hinton 2013).

This point of convergence between business and development on responsive design has led to many buzz phrases, such as "Mobile First", which may excite non-technical stakeholders, yet sadly paint only a part of the bigger picture.

Ethan Marcotte explained how "[o]ur work is defined by its transience, often refined or replaced within a year or two" (Marcotte 2010). It is unfortunate then that businesses now latch onto phraseology that focuses on surface-level solutions, rather than the meaning behind the intent of these techniques.

Right after the dotcom boom, John Allsop addressed a similar situation, chastising our industry for misunderstanding the conditions in which Web design evolves. In his article, he spoke to the fact that designers inherently attempt to control mediums, rather than embrace the circumstances afforded by new ones (Allsop 2000). He argues that the perspectives designers are trained in may end up limiting (business) reality:

> The control which designers know in the print medium, and often desire in the web medium, is simply a function of the limitation of the printed page. We should embrace the fact that the web doesn't have the same constraints, and design for this flexibility.

Conversely, the control that the UI development community knows today through techniques, such as RWD, should not impose constraints on the way businesses approach their digital strategies for the future. Current "responsiveness" is only a small part of what is to be, and the focal point should shift from the way that information looks on devices to how that information is organized across an ecosystem.

Indeed, folks within the wider design community, like Brad Frost, have begun to recognize "the need to develop thoughtful design systems, rather than creating simple collections of web pages" (Frost 2013). This author wholeheartedly agrees.

In my first case study, I examine what I consider a thoughtful design system: presenting ebooks as a sample of how information architecture helps represent information for content consumers engaging in different channels. I argue how content management systems (CMSs) and application programming interfaces (APIs), instead of front-end user interface techniques, reflect a mature model for multi-device usage that enables content creators to disseminate information to different channels at ease. Finally, I illustrate how one information ecosystem has been highly successful and how this is a result of the way they structure their data.

10.2   Case Study: Amazon's Kindle Service

A book, in its common conception, is "a collection of printed pages bound inside a cover (hard or soft) that you could place on a shelf in your library, or in a store" (Ingram 2011).

Books find their history in the physically published form, and, at their most basic, are comprised of pages and typography. They are written by authors and broken down into matter, which is defined by layout. This structure is governed by what is known as the canons of page construction. In short, as Charchar (2010) explains, the canons are a "method [that] existed long before the computer, the printing press and even a defined measuring unit. No picas or points, no inches or millimeters. It can be used with nothing more than a straight edge, a piece of paper and a pencil."

The notion of canons was first explored by typographers J.A. Van de Graaf and Jan Tschichold, yet continues to be examined to this day, with Mark Boulton looking at how "we're designing places for content to flow" in his recent piece, "A New Canon" (Boulton 2012). As it happens though, design has evolved since Tschichold's "The Form of the Book", defined less by the construction of physical properties (like pages) and more by their intangible structure and informational connectedness.When it comes to ebooks, there are no rules to how we produce the perfect "page".

That is, when considering how we represent information in a book today, all those previously defined characteristics—i.e. layout, binding, matter—can be manipulated based on a designer's chosen channel. Take it further, and the underlying structure of a book, such as the author or date of publication, can be embedded within a book as meta-data, whether dictated by a developer or tagged by a user. As expected, the book has begun to be designed in a new way.

But what makes books an interesting example is not how attributes are added to an object, but rather the complexity of presenting information when "publishing" an ebook nowadays. The question arises: do we also include page numbers in text files? How do we choose to hint at presentation on pages? What exactly defines a page nowadays?

What I find most interesting about the ebook is its connection to a decades old conversation in graphic design, a conversation that largely revolves around the importance of form. As Tschichold elucidated (2006),

> It was left to our age to achieve a lively focus on the problem of "form" or design. While up to now form was considered as something external, a product of the "artistic imagination", today we have moved considerably closer to the recognition of its essence through the renewed study of nature and more especially to technology (which is only a kind of second nature). Both nature and technology teach us that "form" is not independent, but grows out of function (purpose), out of the materials used (organic or technical), and out of how they are used.

In the example of ebooks, we start to see the role of structuring information, because a page on a smart phone will undoubtedly be different than a page on a laptop computer. When all is said and done, a book has simply become a medium to deliver content, less defined by its physical components and rather defined by its informational structure—its form.

For example, Amazon's current hardware platform—Fig. 10.2—helps writers publish ebooks by suggesting a format structure. From choosing the format type to enforcing typographic rules, Kindle Direct Publishing allows independent writers to publish books that readers can easily consume on a variety of devices.

Figure 10.2 shows only a handful of the different formats and devices you can read a book through Amazon's Kindle service today.

Here, Kindle is both a hardware platform and a set of cross-device apps. Reading may start in one channel, but could be continued then finished in others. Amazon's ecosystem closely aligns with Resmini and Rosati's definition of cross-channel content consumption (2011), where "the single channel might or might not offer a complete entry point into the ecosystem, but the fact is that most of the users/customers will not stay in that channel from point A to point Z." (Resmini 2012)

Amazon's service model could also be thought of as content shifting (Koczon 2011), where a piece of content identified in one context is made available in another. It is an approach we see many "read it later" companies taking nowadays, with both Pocket and Instapaper having built their entire business on a similar concept.

Pocket and Instapaper are both applications for saving and managing links, acting as tools to set aside articles to read later. Their apps are available in both iOS and Android form, as well as web browser, desktop and ereader formats. You can start with a tweet on your phone, save it, and then return to it in a few hours on your desktop computer and maybe finish on a bus via your tablet the day after.

To these "saving"—or placeholding—service companies, hardware, along with its constrained presentation format, is less important than the structuring of content itself. Instead of grids or textures, what is critical is the way the information is organized in a form that can be recognizable on any device, so as to add value to the

Fig. 10.2 Devices in the Amazon Kindle ecosystem. (Individual images: Amazon.com)

user whatever entry point they may consume the content in. It is about the fluidity of form and strength of device relationships, not page display.

The way we interact with Amazon's devices is premised on the fact that we may or may not actually consume the entirety of information in one place. Devices and their constraints on presentation could be argued to be less important than structure, as it is the way information flows through an ecosystem that provides consumers value.

Furthermore, when it comes to presentation, Amazon's service deals with the aforementioned information representation issue by avoiding the concept of pages altogether. Reading progress is variously reported through the use of locations counters, bars, and timers. In general, to Amazon, the way we represent informational progress on Kindle is secondary to the way that the content is structured. It is the organization of content that matters—a user finds his or her way by navigating the content through structure dependent on the context of usage and the device chosen at the time.

As Mark Boulton contends in "Structure First, Content Always", there has been a shift in the way we both publish and consume content (Boulton 2013). He expounds:

> the model that we took right at the birth of the web form print—the template page and publishing system—is now under attack. It's under attack from the premise that you need to know your content before you can design it. For anyone who's worked in publishing, or had to design a highly scalable branding system, or a wayfinding system, they will know that is nonsense. You don't need Content First. You need Structure First.

A "structure first" approach is a great way of thinking about an ecosystem like Kindle, or other cross-channel services like it. The Kindle ereaders, or services such as Pocket and Instapaper, let anyone take control of content consumption, allowing them where and how they want to consume it, building beautiful seams across devices through the power of formatting. It's like Adam Greenfield described, the role of the ecosystem here is to craft "the seams between the distributed components of a product/service, such that they enhance the perception of the whole." (Greenfield 2007)

Kindle has moved the act of reading to instinctually become an act of multi-device usage, aided by structure. The entire service is enabled mostly by the organization of information, set up by Amazon's overall information architecture.

10.3   Case Study: NPR's Cope System

In his Web 2.0 slide deck, "Life and Times of Flexible Content", published through O'Reilly, Zach Brand details the evolution of NPR's CMS (Brand 2011), a custom back-end that allowed for the uploading, editing, publishing, and modifying of NPR's content.

In his presentation, he explains how content is distributed through different forms after going through the CMS and API, like the .org site or a smartphone app. Once entered in the system, content can end up in places that were not even considered up front, such as a Google Chrome extension or an iGoogle Gadget.

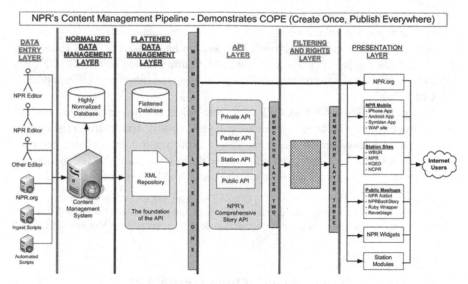

Fig. 10.3 System diagram detailing NPR's COPE. (Jacobson 2009)

While the presentation may seem like a long-winded list, it just goes to show the stretch and reach of NPR's flexible content model. Figure 10.3 below represents the NPR's "Create Once, Publish Everywhere" (COPE) system that enables such content flow.

From a technical perspective, it is what Daniel Jacobson (2009) describes as their content management "pipeline", that is, both a CMS and an API that separates content from display. The system (which handles different types of content, including sound and video) allows for channeling of content through a series of what Brand and Jacobson refer to above as layers. In layers, content can move almost identically regardless of end format or consumer chosen device.

The trajectory of an NPR article may start on the Web, but it could land in many different end locations—even within a native partner app. That is to say, NPR has handled these flexible pieces of content so as to be device agnostic to the point that it even allows for user-generated developments. An example many provide is that of NPR Addict, a fan-built iPhone app that makes approximately 13 years of NPR's content available for browsing and consumption. The coder behind the product—Bradley Flubacher—has no formal relationship to NPR, who thank him on their public blog, and works on his own, outside of NPR's development process.

The app's existence falls largely within Jacobson's description of the system (2009), making it clearly apparent—through practice—that all content from NPR can be remixed. Third parties can reuse posts in any number of different contexts, regardless of their producer's entry form, and create something new out of it.

From a design perspective, what is compelling is how NPR has made flexible choices about presentation hints, for example with different aspect ratio crops on images, to open up opportunities for producers to create for specific environments.

They don't enforce presentation decisions, per se, but they do encourage options that enable anyone to upload for multi-device consumption.

From a business perspective, the NPR's system has produced great returns on investment. User experience designer Karen McGrane detailed how in 2012 NPR's page views increased approximately 80% after implementing the COPE approach (McGrane 2012).

This example of how NPR's COPE came into being, and how it came to structure its information across different presentation layers, vividly demonstrates the crucial role of framing development problems from an information architecture perspective as hardware evolves. In a cross-channel world, solutions are shifting their focus from interface-level approaches to structural ones. As McGrane noted,

> paradoxically, having more structure (…) is going to mean that we're going to have more flexibility in the future to get that content onto places and platforms and devices that we didn't even know would exist when we decided to do this ten years ago. (McGrane 2012)

10.4 Case Study: Facebook's Open Graph API

By September 2012, less than 10 years after it started, Facebook topped over one billion active users (Lee 2012). While the popularization of its service through the media and pop culture undoubtedly played a role in its rise, Facebook's reach can be attributed to the fact that the "Facebook experience" is built to be pervasive, to offer the same experience regardless of device. The development of the Newsfeed, along with the stylization of Facebook posts, point to how the structuring of information helps users understand digital services and come to recognize it as a part of one holistic underlying system.

This possibility is built on Open Graph, Facebook's own API for how users interact with its service and an excellent example of how the structuring of information is an important technique in building up user's mental models of a service.

Open Graph is essentially a model that allows the company to represent data through what it calls "Objects" and "Actions". At its most basic, Open Graph "lets you get information in and out of social media, and helps identify the important elements of a page." (Curtis 2013) In Fig. 10.4 (Chin 2010), Chin illustrates how one user's ("Michael") external interaction creates a graph of information that Facebook and others can understand and derive their own meaning from.

In Open Graph, an object is customarily a single piece of content, such as a petition link (Fig. 10.5), an Instagram photo or a Spotify stream. An "Action", on the other hand, is how a user interacts with that content.

Actions began as an interaction—a "Like"—that a user could carry out through the timeline or Newsfeed, but after "Likes", Facebook began to roll out other user-generated verbs and phrases, a key to their scale when considering the ability to integrate into different places of the Web. "Liking", "sharing a link", "streaming"—

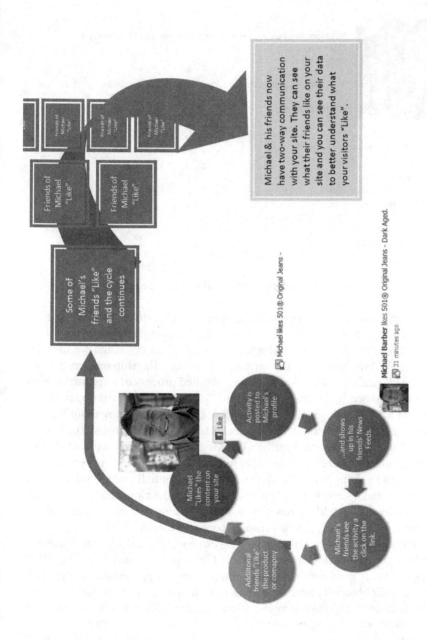

Fig. 10.4 Facebook's open graph. (Chin 2010)

Fig. 10.5 Facebook's open graph protocol

from a non-technical perspective these actually allow users to communicate with a piece of content, thus growing the Facebook service.

Because of actions, Open Graph now connects with outside services, without breaking users' sense of where they are or what they're doing. Unlike the traditional walled gardens of the past, such as Myspace circa 2007, actions reach out to different places on the Web to objects that exist outside of their flagship service. According to Andrea Resmini, "(n)avigation is (an) embodied process of sense making and place making, shaped by language" (Resmini 2013). Perhaps it is the grammar of these custom actions that support the Facebook experience, empowering both the service and its users to interact with what seems to be a ubiquitous environment.

To take it one step forward, Jonathan Waddingham noted back in 2011 that the way Open Graph authorizes other services to model user activities is very close to sentences (Waddingham 2011). He argues how you essentially need to think about what sentences make sense to people when considering development for Facebook. Facebook's information architecture then is about shaping content so that it makes sense to users in different contexts—shaping content through language.

Further, Facebook's objects (i.e. web pages) can come loaded with meta-tags that can later be grouped into similar content pieces (i.e. aggregations) (Arburako 2012). Most simply, this is good organization in practice, since aggregations are grouped according to their objects or actions, such as most played or date viewed.

Facebook actions, objects and aggregations are easily identifiable to every user, which allows for ease of engagement and consumption. It follows that Facebook's Open Graph builds up cognitive fluency—providing lots of new information, through multiple mediums and on multiple devices, without the need to relearn a

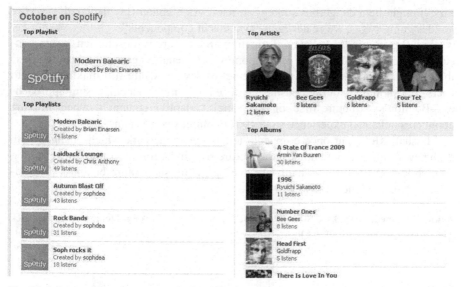

Fig. 10.6 Aggregations in open graph. (Waddingham 2011)

specific format. Cognitive fluency here would be in contrast to cognitive load, i.e. the amount of processing power our brains need to use a system.

As Kathy Whitenton noted, building on existing mental models helps people find content and complete tasks: "(w)hen you use labels and layouts that they've encountered on other websites, you reduce the amount of learning they need to do on your site" (Whitenton 2013). Granted, it's not just websites we're talking about here, but entire cross-channel experiences.

To many, Facebook—and its Open Graph protocol—is just a tool that allows brands (either small businesses or large enterprises) to engage with audiences through a new medium. It would be remiss to focus on its current social media dominance without understanding the way its structured information architecture has contributed to its success (Fig. 10.6).

10.5   Conclusions

Companies like Amazon and NPR illustrate the degrees with which we can begin to shape and reuse content, building up sustainable systems that could be modified for years to come. Facebook proves that organizing information and providing navigational clues through language can lead to a multi-billion-user service.

Today, we often dwell on techniques when discussing the design of systems. However, we should start considering if leading businesses to think of devices (e.g. "mobile") as a defining factor in how they craft digital strategies (e.g. "Mobile

First") might be a dangerous strategy in itself. As Stephen Hay declared, "(w)e're not designing pages, we're designing systems of components".

With this in mind, I believe information architecture is a useful lens when considering the design of systems of components, as it enables content to become flexible, so that it moves through a diverse set of devices while still making sense to users. We should encourage businesses to employ more encompassing approaches—Boulton's "structure first" or McGrane's "adaptive content"—when thinking about cross-channel experience strategy for complex ecosystems.

Marshall McLuhan once quipped: "(i)t is the framework which changes with each new technology and not just the picture within the frame." I fear the definition of mobile will fluctuate as hardware evolves, confusing future business propositions. "Structure" most likely will not.

Acknowledgments Thanks to Stuart Curran, Jeff Wishine, and Chris Ford for providing feedback and ideas on earlier drafts of this piece.

References

Allsop, J. (2000). A Dao of web design. A list apart. http://alistapart.com/article/dao. Accessed Nov 2013.

Arburako. (2012). Facebook open graph. http://www.slideshare.net/arburako/og-13617534. Accessed Nov 2013.

Boulton, M. (2012). A new canon. http://www.markboulton.co.uk/journal/anewcanon. Accessed Dec 2013.

Boulton, M. (2013). Structure first. Content always. http://www.markboulton.co.uk/journal/structure-first-content-always. Accessed Dec 2013.

Brand, Z. (2011). Web 2.0 EXPO. O'Reilly. http://cdn.oreillystatic.com/en/assets/1/event/51/NPR%20Everywhere_%20The%20Power%20of%20Flexible%20Content%20Presentation.pdf. Accessed Nov 2013.

Charchar, A. R. (2010). The secret law of page harmony. Retinart RSS. http://retinart.net/graphic-design/secret-law-of-page-harmony/. Accessed Jan 2014.

Chin, M. (2010). Facebook's key to success-Open API? Just NMT & Cindy :). http://blogs.murdoch.edu.au/cindychin/201. Accessed Feb 2014.

Curtis, H. (2013). 5 most important semantic markups for your website. The Design Studio. http://www.theedesign.com/blog/2013/5-most-important-semantic-markups-for-your-website. Accessed Jan 2014.

Frost, B. (2013). Atomic design. Brad Frost Web. http://bradfrostweb.com/blog/post/atomic-web-design. Accessed Dec 2013.

Greenfield, A. (2007). On the ground running: Lessons from experience design. Speedbird. http://speedbird.wordpress.com/2007/06/22/on-the-ground-running-lessons-from-experience-design/. Accessed Jan 2014.

Hinton, A. (2013). Is it stating the obvious to say "responsive web design" is a valuable technique, but it's not a strategy? If not, let's state is more. https://twitter.com/inkblurt/status/316278804307910657. Accessed Mar 2013.

Ingram, M. (2011). What is a book? The definition continues to blur-tech news and analysis. Gigaom.   http://gigaom.com/2011/04/22/what-is-a-book-the-definition-continues-to-blur/. Accessed Jan 2014.

Jacobson, D. (2009). Programmable web. COPE: Create once, publish everywhere. http://blog. programmableweb.com/2009/10/13/cope-create-once-publish-everywhere/. Accessed Nov 2013.

Koczon, C. (2011). Orbital content. A list apart. http://alistapart.com/article/orbital-content. Accessed Nov 2013.

Lee, D. (2012). Facebook surpasses one billion users as it tempts new markets. BBC News. http://www.bbc.co.uk/news/technology-19816709. Accessed Dec 2013.

Marcotte, E. (25 May 2010). Responsive web design. A list apart. http://alistapart.com/article/responsive-web-design/. Accessed 13 Jan 2014.

McGrane, K. (2012). Adapting ourselves to adaptive content. http://karenmcgrane.com/2012/09/04/adapting-ourselves-to-adaptive-content-video-slides-and-transcript-oh-my/. Accessed Jan 2014.

Roberts, A. (2014). Media Queries—SitePoint. SitePoint. Retrieved June 22, 2014, from http://www.sitepoint.com/web-foundations/media-queries/.

Pins, M., & Hild, H. (2013). Image based artistic dithering. http://www.visgraf.impa.br/Courses/ip00/proj/Dithering1/. Accessed Jan 2014.

Resmini, A. (2012). What is cross-channel? http://andrearesmini.com/blog/what-is-cross-channel. Accessed Dec 2013.

Resmini, A. (2013). *Ghost in the shell-navigation, meaning and placemaking in information space*. Proceedings of the international UDC seminar on classification and visualization 2013. http://www.udcds.com/seminar/2013/media/slides/aresmini_udcseminar2013.pdf. Accessed Dec 2013.

Resmini, A. & Rosati, L. (2011). *Pervasive information architecture-designing cross-channel user experiences*. Burlington: Morgan Kauffman.

Tschichold, J. (2006). The new typography (New ed.). Berkeley, Calif.: University of California Press.

Waddingham, J. (2011). Waddingham's words (and pics). hhttp://jonathanwaddingham.com/2011/10/29/grammar-as-a-platform-and-sentences-as-a-service-facebooks-new-open-graph/. Accessed Dec 2013.

Whitenton, K. (2013). Minimize cognitive load to maximize usability. Nielsen Norman Group. http://www.nngroup.com/articles/minimize-cognitive-load/. Accessed Dec 2013.

Chapter 11
Cross-channel Design for Cultural Institutions—The Istituto degli Innocenti in Florence

Luca Rosati, Antonella Schena and Rita Massacesi[1]

Abstract The paper illustrates the way a cultural institution can embrace a systemic and cross-channel approach that enables it to link together a number of different entities and sources of knowledge on childhood and adolescence, which it owns. These channels are related one to another to create a unique ecosystem, to allow a seamless experience among various contexts and a systemic integration of the institution's holdings. The relationship between different channels is brought about through the use of a thesaurus; navigation between the terms in the thesaurus allows the creation of a consistent structure of relationships between the channels. The thesaurus makes it possible to move from the digital channels of the organization (website, OPAC, digital repository) to the physical ones (library, museum, or archive) using specific subjects as a compass; to pursue the visit experience by choosing specific paths within the physical space or to move from the physical to the digital world; and to develop an integrated use of web resources during a visit in physical space in order to customize the path and find objects or related information.

11.1 Introduction

The case described in this article arises from two distinct but linked purposes:

- the desire to provide people with a consistent information journey and experience across the heterogeneous channels and touch-points of the organization;

This work is the result of a collaborative effort; however, Luca Rosati wrote Introduction, Cross-channel user journey, The museum and the archive, Conclusions; Antonella Schena wrote Towards a common ground of Knowledge about Childhood and Adolescence; and Rita Massacesi Application of the thesaurus in the cross-channel strategy. The case study has also been documented in Rosati et al. (2013).

L. Rosati (✉)
Information Architect, Perugia, Italy
e-mail: luca@lucarosati.it

A. Schena · R. Massacesi
Istituto degli Innocenti, Firenze, Italy

A. Resmini (ed.), *Reframing Information Architecture,* Human-Computer Interaction Series, 145
DOI 10.1007/978-3-319-06492-5_11, © Springer International Publishing Switzerland 2014

Fig 11.1 The Istituto degli Innocenti is hosted in the ancient structure of the Ospedale degli Innocenti, designed by Filippo Brunelleschi in the fifteenth century. (Source: Aurelio Candido, Flickr)

- the desire to create and disseminate a multifaceted, integrated knowledge of childhood as a condition, referring either to our contemporary society or in a historical perspective

These desires are a consequence of the specific nature and mandate of the Istituto degli Innocenti, which has been carrying out activities relating to the protection of children's rights for centuries. Founded in Florence in the first half of the 15th century as a place for the assistance and care of abandoned children, the Istituto degli Innocenti (Fig. 11.1) is now a service center supporting a number of diversified activities. Among these:

- it carries out documentation, research, and training activities for the National Childhood and Adolescence Documentation and Analysis Centre of the Italian government (http://www.minori.it) and for the Regional Childhood and Adolescence Documentation Centre of the Regione Toscana (http://www.minori.toscana.it);
- it manages educational and care services for children and mothers in need;
- it holds a precious historical archive;
- it manages a library, the Innocenti Library Alfredo Carlo Moro;
- it hosts a significant artistic heritage, which will become more accessible to the public through the new museum, the Museo degli Innocenti (MUDI).

In order to link these different entities and knowledge sources on childhood and adolescence, which developed separately over a long period of time, the organization

Fig. 11.2 The cross-channel strategy for the Istituto degli Innocenti. The thesaurus acts as a bonding agent capable to link together the hetero-geneous channels of the organization

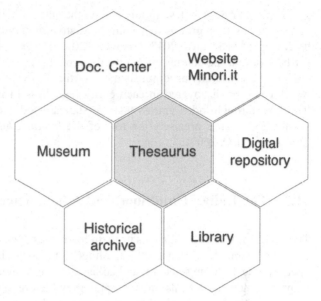

has tested a working method based on a systemic and cross-channel approach (Res-mini and Rosati 2011; Rosati 2006). The aim was to initiate a transition from a "si-los" logic (or at least a juxtapositional one) to an ecosystem one, where the institute is considered in its complex entirety. The relationship between these different chan-nels was created on a semantic basis through the use of a controlled vocabulary, the *Italian Childhood and Adolescence Thesaurus* (ThIA 2007). Navigation between the terms in the thesaurus, linked to the individual resources, allowed the creation of a consistent and repeatable structure of relationships between them, able to guide users in their research (Fig. 11.2).

11.2   Towards Common Grounds for Knowledge About Childhood and Adolescence

In Italy, as in other countries, the differences between cultural institutions (librar-ies, archives, and museums) are beginning to disappear, overcoming in this way the limits due to the fragmentation of the cultural heritage sector. As a result, it has been necessary to reframe the procedures and methods used in intellectual work and for the spreading of knowledge, also considering the fact that these processes increas-ingly take place in a digital dimension and in a web arena. There is a great deal of debate on the development of new methods and tools for the creation of integrated and straightforward access to data coming from different areas (Latham 2012; Res-mini and Rosati 2011; Gnoli 2007, 2010; Rosati 2006).

One of the most debated questions is, on one hand, the need to safeguard the identity of the individual areas of production of this data, which reference different standards and rules for description; and on the other, to keep in mind the real needs of the various user groups to whom alternative methods of data collection have been proposed (Scaturro 2013; Giannetto 2011; Doerr et al. 2008). In this context, we believe that the sharing of knowledge coming from different descriptive systems could be usefully accomplished by starting from a common semantic ground, which could be discovered in each entity regardless of its originating field, and, therefore, through index entries that are standardized and framed in a controlled vocabulary. That is precisely the role of the *Italian Childhood and Adolescence Thesaurus* (ThIA 2007).

11.3   The Italian Childhood and Adolescence Thesaurus

The thesaurus was built taking as its main reference the standard ISO 2788-1986 for the building and development of monolingual thesauri. The vocabulary was developed starting with the selection and collection of terminology used to index documents (articles, periodicals, monographs, grey literature, audiovisual material) by the National and Regional Documentation Centre based on an inductive, bottom-up methodology. The thesaurus in the 2007 print version was made up of 2953 preferred terms; it is constantly enriched and updated. In the online version, in addition to the display of the whole hierarchical structure and the navigation of relationships, it was also possible to create an interface with the catalogue of the documentation centers and permit navigation between the thesaurus terms, the subject strings, and the linked documents.

From a structural point of view, the main features of the thesaurus are: the building methodology that follows a mixed method (organization both in thematic areas and in facets)—this method is permitted by norm ISO 2788, 9.3.2; and polyhierarchy, that is, the possibility for some terms to have links to more than one broader term.

Therefore, the vocabulary is divided into two levels: the first one, consisting of seven thematic areas (Culture, Education, Childhood and Adolescence, Institutions, Psychological processes, Health, Society) fixes the systemic structure; the second one, the faceted level, fixes the classification structure of the individual terms within the areas.

The use of polyhierarchy is strictly linked to this organization. As a matter of fact, the decision to organize the terminology into thematic areas allowed topics concerning childhood and adolescence to be put inside a specific multidisciplinary area (childhood and adolescence), so that terms linked to this particular conceptual field are located within a specific and extended semantic network (see box below).

In the *Italian Childhood and Adolescence Thesaurus* the term Tribunale per i minorenni (Juvenile Court) is located both in:

Infanzia e adolescenza [Childhood and adolescence, thematic area]
— [Organi giudiziari minorili]
   - Tribunale per i minorenni

and in:

Istituzioni [Institutions, thematic area]
— [Tribunali]
   - Tribunale per i minorenni

Alongside the main area, other different structures were developed, within which the terms linked to childhood and adolescence are located within the specific hierarchies of the different classification structures. Though polyhierarchy relates mainly to the childhood and adolescence area, it can also affect other areas.

To build structures within the thematic areas, a categorical analysis of the terms was used in order to indicate, for each term, the main category to which it belongs (e.g., actions, actors, things), and, within it, the division features – that is, the facets (see box below).

The thematic area Educazione (Education) is divided in:

— [Education according to the recipients] i.e. implicit facet
   - Educazione degli adulti
   - Educazione familiare
— [Education according to the method] (i.e. implicit facet)
   - Educativa territoriale
   - Educazione non formale
   - etc.

The identification of the main macro-categories was also essential for verifying the terms. As a matter of fact, the terms selected for the vocabulary were submitted to a rigorous analysis in order to obtain homogeneity and univocity in the language from a formal and semantic point of view, so that each term can express one and only one idea, and vice versa an idea is expressed always by one and only one term, getting rid of the ambiguities of natural language (ThIA 2007, pp. 11–35).

In this process, the constant reference was also the Subject Indexing Guide by GRIS (the research group on subject indexing of the Italian Libraries Association), especially for the interaction between the semantic and the syntactic parts of the indexing language and its implications for the building of the vocabulary (AIB GRIS 2001).

11.4 Cross-channel User Journey

While working on the re-design of the National Childhood and Adolescence Documentation and Analysis Centre website, we noticed the close interrelation of this area with the other documentation spheres of the Istituto degli Innocenti (the museum, the archive, and the library). Then the idea came to link them together. More precisely, the idea is to create a series of informative paths that cross the different channels and traverse from digital to physical space and vice versa. In the end, there was both the opportunity and the need to plan a pervasive and cross-channel information architecture (Resmini & Rosati, 2011; Rosati 2006) able to link together the different activity areas of the organization (Fig. 11.2).

The basic idea is that the different activities of the Istituto degli Innocenti function as touch points for the same service, so that the user's journey can start from any of the different points and can go on in a consistent and fluid way through to any other contact point – the website, the library, the museum, or vice versa, without a break from the point of view of the enrichment, extension, and variety of the visiting experience.

This plan is supported by:

- the idea of information and user journey, that is to say the strategic value of the paths conceived in a cross-channel key (Blandford & Attfield, 2010), and
- the thesaurus as the bonding agent in this pervasive architecture, where it is transversally applied to all the channels of the Istituto degli Innocenti.

Regarding this latter point, those channels (such as the museum) that do not use the thesaurus in a systematic way could also easily make use of it. As it is a structure made of keywords (or tags – to use Web 2.0 terminology), the thesaurus allows tagging not only of web resources, but also of archival documents, museum objects or paths, and library materials and services, establishing the possibility of passing from one to the other through the hierarchical or associative relationships of a term with nearby ones. RFId, QR codes, and mobile devices allow these paths to be easily created in the physical world as well and to get them onto their digital counterparts (Resmini & Rosati, 2010).

11.5 Application of the Thesaurus in the Cross-Channel Strategy

11.5.1 The Website Minori.it

In order to apply a controlled vocabulary such as the Childhood and Adolescence Thesaurus to the web, it was necessary to make some modifications for more streamlined and user-friendly navigation, and also to gear it to unskilled users. The changes involved both structural and terminological levels, including the facets

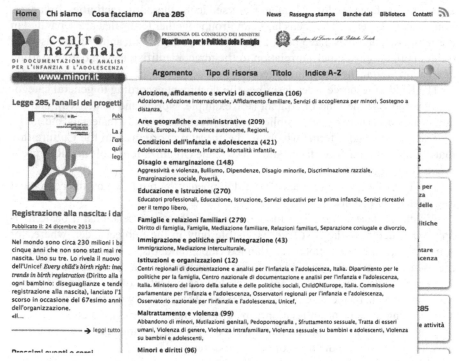

Fig. 11.3 The main navigation of the website Minori.it is based on the same semantic structure of the thesaurus, with some adaptations (the facets are brought to the foreground)

clarification and the reduction of the levels in the hierarchy. In the web version of the vocabulary, the seven thematic areas have been removed, and the facets have been brought to the foreground. The clarification of the faceted structure allows for better navigation as a whole, through

- combining the focus of the facets—in the same way as with tag structure, to which many users are used, and
- correlating similar resources with focuses in common—so that the detailed file for a resource in the website suggests other semantically related resources.

In the new website, three main facets have been singled out: *subject*, ordering documents on the basis of their content; *kind of resource*, ordering documents on the basis of the kind of publication; *titles*, ordering documents on the basis of their own titles or the titles of the collections (Fig. 11.3).

Each facet represents an independent vocabulary for the user that nevertheless shares terminology and basic structure with the thesaurus, apart from the third facet, which includes the title of the document described or of the collection.

The Subject facet is the core of the system. All of its terms come from the childhood and adolescence field and have been gathered together in 15 foci (Adoption, Foster care and reception services; Education, Learning and Educational services, etc.), which refer to the logical categories used in the thesaurus (activities, organizations, processes, etc.). The focus tags can group together terms that are separated in the thesaurus, and they have been conceived to be highly meaningful for users in order to offer them a quick correlation to the topic, identifiable even before starting navigation among the subordinate terms.

The Kind of resource facet describes the document according to general categories that indicate the kind of content (for example, Norms and sentences), and the aim or function (for example, Bibliography, Meetings or study materials, etc.).

This facet includes terms which, in the thesaurus, originate in the Culture thematic field, Cultural Tools facct, and Knowledge Organization Tools and Representation Tools sub-facets.

The Titles facet includes the titles of documentation produced by the center and any related collections.

Within the facets, there is a moderate use of thesaurus relations; a basic hierarchical structure at the first level is visible only in the Subject facet, where, for some terms, explanatory notes are planned (though not displayed now), so that, for the users, their meaning and indexing use is always clear. In the future, it could be interesting to develop a system able to exploit the potential of the associative relationships, which, by reciprocal linking of terms that have very strict interchangeable and meaning superposition relationships among them, seems to be closest to free tagging, but without risking an uncontrolled expansion of the set of search terms, which was devised on the basis of accurate criteria.

11.5.2   The Museum and the Archive

The need to create a connection between these different channels was particularly relevant due to the creation of the new museum. The museum, apart from collecting the works of artists that have made this reception space beautiful and unique, aims to create virtual online exhibitions and thematic paths in order to tell the history of the Istituto degli Innocenti, and of its activities, linking together documents of different natures and origins (from archival documents to the most recent contributions linked to new documentary activities).

To support the user during the visit, next to traditional analogue equipment (banners, texts, audio-visuals), the new museum plans to use RFID systems and portable devices with net connections, through which integrative digital content can be viewed, along with the opportunity to customize the visit path (Mandelli et al. 2011).

Highly significant for the realization of these projects are the sources coming from the historical archive. The relevance of its heritage lies in the uniqueness of the pieces and in the consideration that many archive series have a chronological continuity that allows significant research over long periods of time. At the moment, consultation of the archive is possible through its online inventory, which allows users to navigate among funds, sections, sectors, and information cards, making them understand the complexity of the hierarchical structure (thanks also to the graphical display of the results). The semantic indexes which will allow subject access have not been created yet. In the next paragraph, we will see that some archival materials have been indexed in an experimental way with descriptors coming from the thesaurus, with the prospect of integration between different information channels, as described so far, or to offer to archive users also the possibility of content access.

11.5.3   The Children of Italy Exhibition and the Digital Repository

The exhibition *Children of Italy: The Innocents and the birth of a childhood national project (1861–1911)*—open from December 3, 2011 to June 3, 2012—has been a first test of the approach described so far. The exhibition traces the history of the Istituto degli Innocenti and the development of national childhood policies in the first 50 years following Italian unification. Through the biographies of some of the children who lived in the Institute (and in other Italian charitable institutions between 1861 and 1911), old pictures, objects, videos, and archival documents, the daily life of children inside the institutes is recounted; the evolution of their reception, their care, and education, the demographic aspects and the life paths that awaited them in the new nation, the care for pregnant women. Information-rich legends support and accompany the archive documents and the 40 photos on display, coming from the historical Archive of the Istituto and from other important collections. A report of this event was published on the center's website and gave rise to the opportunity to analyze the topic of child abandonment and care not only from a historical perspective, but also with a look at the condition of children in contemporary society.

The experimentation leading to a cross-channel thematic path starts from here, from the desire to give the users the chance of finding an organized and navigable knowledge space on the topics discussed in the web article.

The first step was the classification of the website page according to the thesaurus. According to the analysis, the document shows itself to be a news report that analyses the topics of child abandonment, the condition of children outside of the family, and reception services. Apart from these main concepts, it is possible to identify other topics that, even though they are not principal, have definite relevance to the main topic (such as, for example, family foster care; the history of the Istituto; the daily life of children inside institutes; and so on). Thus, the main topics are expressed through the *Subject, Kind of resource, Titles* facets discussed above. Navigating the facets will allow the users to conduct their searches inside the site, widening or limiting according to well thought out, non-random procedures.

Beyond the facets, a set of contextual links (based on the subject statement) allows more cross-channel connections. These links will lead the user out of the site, putting him in contact with different information channels, where his search can be deepened or reoriented: for example, bibliographies or filmographies in the Institute OPAC (http://opac.minori.it), thematic visual reference desk, or digitized documents from the museum or archive. In relation to the topic discussed, these last

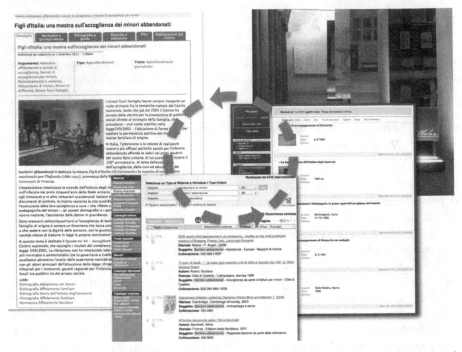

Fig 11.4 An example of cross-channel user journey according to the thematic path of "abandoned children": from the website report to the OPAC to the digital repository to the museum; and vice versa

materials are of particular interest. These materials are managed through the digital repository, a preservation tool for digitized materials developed by a group of Italian companies specializing in the field of digitalization and kindly offered so that this application could be tested.

Inside the repository were put some museum objects and archival documents, which were appropriately digitized and linked to the topics dealt with in the news report from which we started, including a digitized reproduction of a painting (the Madonna degli Innocenti); a picture (the reinforced window of the Istituto degli Innocenti); archival documents (the history of Demetrio).

Moreover, through the same thesaurus terms, it will be possible to travel from the digital channels (website, OPAC, digital repository) to the physical ones (the library, the museum, the archive), not in a generic way but having as a compass specific subjects—those of the thesaurus in its web adaptation—corresponding to specific paths or artifacts inside the buildings (Fig. 11.4).

Inside the repository, the physical characteristics of the materials were described and they were indexed using the thesaurus terms. The user can enter the repository from the web by starting from one of the terms used in the Subject facet to describe the news report, and can find, in this way, a series of documents with similar content; once inside the repository, it is possible to navigate via the thesaurus terms to refine the search.

In a similar way it is possible to conceive an equal and opposite path switching from the physical sphere to the digital one. Alternately, the integrated use of digital resources inside the physical places can be applied in order to customize the paths, to find a specific item, or to receive more information about it.

11.6 Conclusions

In this paper we have seen how different channels and contexts (different in their nature, functions and interface) could be related one to another to create a unique ecosystem, exploiting a common information architecture, so as to allow a continuity of experience among various contexts and a systematic integration of the activities and faces of an organization.

The basis for this process is a product of the documentation field: the thesaurus. It can become the tool that can help further an overall knowledge of the actions and of the topics concerning childhood and adolescence, both from a historical perspective, and as a contemporary life condition.

Using the thesaurus tools, moreover, it will be possible to move from the digital channels of the Istituto degli Innocenti (the website, the OPAC, the digital repository) to the physical ones (such as the library, the museum or the archive), but not only in a generic way, on the contrary with specific subjects as a compass—subjects expressed through the *Italian Childhood and Adolescence Thesaurus* terms (or those adapted for the web). In this way, it will be possible to pursue the visit experience by choosing specific paths within the physical space, or, vice versa, it will be possible to move from the physical to the digital world. More than that, through mobile devices, it will be possible to develop an integrated use of web resources during a visit in physical space, in order to customize paths, and find objects or related information. The next step after correlation within a single channel is correlation across channels, among resources and paths that span physical and digital space.

References

AIB GRIS. (2001). Guida all'indicizzazione per soggetto (Subject indexing guide). AIB Rome. http://www.sba.unifi.it/mod-Areafiles-display-lid-308-cid-79.html. Accessed Jan 2014.
Blandford, A., & Attfield, S. (2010). *Interacting with information*. London: Morgan & Claypool.
Doerr, M., Bekiari, C., & LeBoeuf, P. (2008). *FRBRoo, a conceptual model for performing arts*. In The digital curation of cultural heritage. Proceedings of the ICOM-CIDOC Annual Meeting 2008 (http://www.ics.forth.gr/_publications/drfile.2008-06-42.pdf).
Giannetto, M. (2011). *Mostre virtuali online. Linee guida per la realizzazione: la genesi di un progetto per il web culturale* (Online virtual exhibitions: guidelines). *DigItalia, 6*(1), 147–160 (http://digitalia.sbn.it/article/view/498).

Gnoli, C. (2007). *La biblioteca semantica* (The semantic library). Milano: Editrice Bibliografica.

Gnoli, C. (2010). Classification transcends library business. *Knowledge Organization, 37*(3), 223–229.

Latham, K. F. (2012). Museum object as document: Using Buckland's information concepts to understand museum experiences. *Journal of Documentation, 68*(1), 45–71.

Mandelli, E., Resmini, A., & Rosati, L. (2011) *Architettura dell'informazione e design museale* (Information architecture and museum design). *Tafter Journal, 37.* http://www.tafterjournal. it/2011/07/01/architettura-dell%E2%80%99informazione-e-design-museale/.

Resmini, A., & Rosati, L. (2010). *The semantic environment: Heuristics for a cross-context human-information interaction model.* In Dubois, E., Gray, P., & Nigay, L. (Eds.), *The engineering of mixed reality systems* (pp. 79–100). New York: Springer.

Resmini, A., & Rosati, L. (2011). *Pervasive information architecture: Designing cross-channel user experiences.* Morgan Kaufmann. ·

Rosati, L. (2006). *Architettura dell'informazione: Trovabilità dagli oggetti quotidiani al Web* (Information architecture: From everyday things to the Web). Apogeo.

Rosati, L., Schena, A., & Massacesi, R. (2013). Childhood and adolescence between past and present. *Knowledge Organization, 40*(3), 197–204.

Scaturro, I. (2013). Faceted taxonomies for the performing arts domain: the case of the european collected library of artistic performance. *Knowledge Organization, 40*(3), 205–211.

ThIA. (2007). *Thesaurus italiano Infanzia e Adolescenza* (Italian childhood and adolescence thesaurus). Firenze: Istituto degli Innocenti (http://www.minori.it/thesaurus).

Printed in the United States
By Bookmasters